THE LITTLE
UPHOLSTERY
BOOK | SHELLY MILLER LEER

A Beginner's Guide to Artisan Upholstery

SCHIFFER PUBLISHING

4880 Lower Valley Road • Atglen, PA 19310

Published by Schiffer Publishing, Ltd.
4880 Lower Valley Road
Atglen, PA 19310
Phone: (610) 593-1777; Fax: (610) 593-2002
E-mail: Info@schifferbooks.com
Web: www.schifferbooks.com

For our complete selection of fine books on this and related subjects, please visit our website at www.schifferbooks.com. You may also write for a free catalog.

Schiffer Publishing's titles are available at special discounts for bulk purchases for sales promotions or premiums. Special editions, including personalized covers, corporate imprints, and excerpts, can be created in large quantities for special needs. For more information, contact the publisher.

We are always looking for people to write books on new and related subjects. If you have an idea for a book, please contact us at proposals@schifferbooks.com.

With loving dedication to my late sister, Marsha, a master and lover of the written word. She possessed a lightning-fast mind, boundless creativity, and the most cleverly wonderful sense of humor. I envied her intellect much.

Every artist was first an amateur.

—Ralph Waldo Emerson

Contents

Foreword

Have you ever had a seemingly small experience trigger a big change in your life? This happened to me ten years ago, when, during an early morning run through my neighborhood, I saw an old chair perched on the curb as it waited for the day's trash pickup.

The Queen Anne–style antique was torn to pieces, with seat springs hanging out of the bottom, but it had a regal, curved back that commanded attention and deserved a better fate than the landfill. I returned with my car and hauled it home. Every few weeks I'd look at it in my garage, not knowing what to do with it but having an inkling that I wanted to learn how to reupholster it.

A few months later, after seeing an ad for an upholstery class in New York City, I found myself driving two hours every Saturday from my home outside Philadelphia to hammer nails into a piece of wood and tie Italian twine onto coil springs. My hands were cut and raw from practicing, but I was hooked and knew I wanted to start my own upholstery business restoring chairs.

When the class ended, I still didn't know enough to open my own shop, so I applied to be a forty-year-old intern at a furniture company in Philadelphia. I opened the doors to Wild Chairy four months later, never believing anyone would actually buy something that I made with my own two hands.

Whether your goal in learning to upholster is to acquire a creative hobby, start a side business, or simply breathe new life into an outdated or neglected piece like the Cinderella chair I found on the curb, you will delight in this essential yet friendly primer by Shelly Leer. I wish it had been available when I was tackling my first project! By pairing easy-to-follow instructions with generous photos and images that help you check your work as you go along, Shelly has created a book that will have you feeling confident, creative, and, above all, *competent* in no time—all without spending weeks in a class or an internship.

What makes *The Little Upholstery Book* so good for beginners is that it avoids information overload, reflecting Shelly's understanding that there is beauty in the basics. After teaching upholstery to hundreds of students, she saw how novices flourish best when the focus is on fundamental skills that can be applied to almost every project. She makes upholstering inspiring, not intimidating, and that translates into projects you'll actually finish. As for the pride you'll feel at what you've accomplished—well, I'll just call that the "chairy" on top!

Besides this book, Shelly shares her expertise through blogs, social media, and even upholstery boot camps. I personally enjoy being part of her Instagram and Facebook communities: I love seeing what others create, and I hope to see your first project created with the help of *The Little Upholstery Book* there, too!

—Andrea Mihalik, owner, Wild Chairy

Acknowledgments

A BIG THANK YOU TO:

Matt Leer, my creative, writer son who was always cheering for me when I needed it. Our Sunday evening phone calls motivated me to persevere and be brave enough to use my own voice.

John Leer, my kind and intellectual son who never doubted that I could write a book. Where'd you come from, anyway?

Anna Leer, my high-achieving daughter who got me to understand the rewards of setting big goals.

Anne Miller, my dear sister-in-law who listened to me rant about everything on our Sunday morning walks and brunch. Sisters for life.

My Beloved Miller Family: Mike, Patty, Nate, Shelly, Drew, Owen, Lizzy, and Beau. You are gold to me.

Elliott Miller, my creative nephew who always keeps me on my artistic toes.

My friends, who have patiently waited for me to finish this project. These folks lift me up and continue to make me a better person.

Jan Distel, the best moral support a person could ever have. She's the closest thing to having a mom who always sees the good in everything.

Griffon Fabrics, the ladies who are always willing to stop and help when you need it.

Schiffer Publishing and their former senior editor, *Doug Congdon-Martin*, who listened to more than a few ambitious pitches of mine during lunch in Port Townsend, Washington, at the Furniture Design Society's annual conference. Thanks for listening and believing that I had a new take on this subject.

Introduction

The Fresh New Face of Upholstery

After years of teaching upholstery to hundreds of eager students, I started to notice a trend emerging from a new generation of tech-savvy, bright, and ambitious men and women. Whether they're tired of their corporate jobs or exhausted by clocking endless hours working for other small-business owners, this wave of workers is longing for the tangible satisfaction of working with their hands. The booming interest in artisan crafts and skills is a testament to the human need to make things.

Traditional and modern upholstery have caught the attention of an emerging crop of new upholsterers, who appreciate the process of learning a specialized skill and utilizing existing, well-made furniture, as well as applying their own artistic spin to the craft. The model of "ye olde upholstery shop" is gradually fading and being replaced with fresh, new, creative hybrids owned and operated according to a new playbook.

Which brings us to the title of this book—*The Little Upholstery Book: A Beginner's Guide to Artisan Upholstery.*

This upholstery book is unlike any other on the market. The information and projects have been mindfully designed to teach professional upholstery skills in a simplified, easy-to-understand manner that will empower you with the confidence to get started right away on your exciting, practical, and creative journey. Whether you're doing contract work for clients or redesigning vintage furniture for sale, or you have an irresistible desire to learn upholstery for your own enjoyment, *The Little Upholstery Book* is a hands-on field guide you'll want by your side as you build your skills. I've gathered and honed twenty-five years of my upholstery knowledge, experience, and lessons learned to help you find your own rewarding path.

*Upholstery can change your life, if you let it.
—Miss Mamie Hammonds, upholstery teacher, southern lady, and woman of wisdom*

From setting up your workspace to shooting your first staple, the skills and techniques you'll learn as you complete the following projects can be practiced, adapted, and utilized to help you begin earning money immediately. Besides learning how to upholster like a pro, this practical, centuries-old craft brings with it a sense of deep, soul-satisfying creative accomplishment.

Believe it or not, it won't take long before clients come knocking on your door with a piece of furniture and a willingness to pay you for your special skills. Tackling the simple jobs in the first exciting days of your new venture shouldn't scare you. You'll be presented with valuable opportunities to earn while you learn. This model worked for me as I was learning my craft and raising three young children. There was very little time to practice without the pressing need to earn extra cash for a growing family.

You'll feel better about your business, as well as less pressure, if you can finance this venture yourself, so as not to have to borrow money. This book is a blueprint for you.

I would have a workshop attached
to every school, and one hour a
day given up to the teaching of
simple decorative arts. It would
be a golden hour to the children.

—Oscar Wilde

section one

Getting Set Up

Chapter One

THE WORKSHOP

A HOME WORKSHOP

Welcome to the centuries-old craft of upholstery. Whether you're learning this skill for the sheer sake of learning something new, or for its valuable and practical application, you need a place to work. Just about any room in a house or apartment can double as your upholstery "shop." As you progress, you'll eventually want your own space away from common living areas. Starting out, it's wise to keep your costs low. To get up and running right away, let's find a space that will work for you.

A happy home makes a happy upholsterer.

Upholstery work is messy. A clean, bright, and organized shop helps productivity and can make spending your time there more enjoyable. Due to the time it takes to upholster a piece of furniture from start to finish, it makes sense to tidy up cuttings and messes at the end of a day's work, but you'll also want to be able to leave projects out until your next work session. Trying to work right in the middle of shared spaces may cause frustration and resentment from housemates. No matter where you're working, be respectful of the people with whom you're sharing space. You'll want to keep your loved ones happy with your work-from-home arrangement.

It's best to start by carving out a little-used space in your house. The logical places to set up a home shop are in the garage, the basement, a spare bedroom, or an extra room that gets little use. I started out in the basement but occasionally had to tear down large pieces in the dining room. I later expanded to the garage, went back to the basement when I started teaching classes, and then moved to a spacious 1,990-square-foot leased shop. Start small and see how your business grows.

YOUR SPACE WILL NEED TO INCLUDE THE FOLLOWING:

Cutting table (I used a ping-pong table for over twenty years)
Work surfaces, such as sawhorses and low rolling tables
Storage for materials, tools, needles, pins, and notions
Tool surfaces, such as small rolling carts and countertops
Wide doors with room to get furniture in and out
Plenty of light and electrical outlets
A powerful fan / air conditioning for hot days and heat for cold days
Open floor space with room to walk around
Surface for a computer, books, writing, desktop, and chair
Pull-up stool

Sawhorses are a staple of an upholstery shop. Determine what your needs are as far as height, whether you want a lipped-top surface, and if you need storage below the top surface. Then, look for the right instructions—there are plenty available. To save time and money, there are basic horses available at big-box home improvement stores that can be customized to meet your needs.

If you have space in your home that fits the bill, then you're ready to equip it with the necessary tools and materials. If you'll be looking for away-from-home space, keep these requirements in mind.

YOUR VERY OWN LEASED SHOP

Less is better. Shop expenses eat up profits. However, if you decide to lease space, make a wish list of everything you'd like it to include. As you begin looking at different spaces, compare the costs and determine which things you absolutely need, and which things you can do without in order to stay within your budget.

Location: A shop that gets a good amount of foot traffic is always beneficial. When potential customers see your sign and shop every day on their way to work, chances are they'll contact you when they need an upholsterer. On the other hand, you may want your shop to be out of the way so that you're not interrupted during the workday.

Size: If you choose a shop front, you'll need to plan out necessary work areas to ensure maximum productivity. You'll need space for cutting tables, sawhorses or low supports for work in progress, an area for sewing, storage cabinets or shelves, *lighting, lighting, lighting*, and a bathroom. You may prefer to meet with customers at their location, or you may want to provide a nice sitting area where your customers can look at your fabrics and go over designs and costs.

The Search: Where do you even start looking for space? Check out Craigslist or a local newspaper, let friends know what you're looking for, and ask realtor friends if they know of any commercial space available. Get the word out that you're looking for space for your business. People love to help someone who's starting their own business.

Oftentimes, a friend or family member steps up and offers you space to work, free of charge. If that's the case, be sure to discuss each and every aspect of your arrangement ahead of time so that you're not caught by surprise when they boot you out when their son comes back to live at home and needs the space. It behooves everyone to understand all expectations up front—in writing, if possible.

Once you find the shop space of your dreams, there are a number of expenses that might catch you by surprise, because, let's face it, the thrill of getting your very own workspace can be blinding. Be wise from the very beginning; understand and document where every penny of your hobby or business enters and exits your bank account. Monthly bills roll around before you know it. Understanding monthly and seasonal workflow is necessary for budgeting during slower times of the year. Impeccable management of cash flow in a business like ours can mean the difference between succeeding or failing.

Expenses

Planning and equipping your shop with shelves, extra lighting, a working bathroom, furniture for customers or visitors, and a small kitchen area takes money. You can save lots of money by using recycled building materials, used furniture, and even small, used kitchen appliances such as a mini refrigerator and microwave. A coat of paint does wonders for a space (surprise, surprise!).

HERE ARE SOME OF THE COSTS YOU NEED TO PLAN FOR WHEN YOU LEASE SPACE:

Rent
Utilities
Insurance
Signage
Local taxes on exterior signage
Alarm system
Phone line for WiFi
Retrofitting doors for moving big pieces in and out
Fresh paint
HVAC (heating, ventilation, and air conditioning)
Any build-out you need

Most of these are not one-time expenses—they'll be due each and every month. Crunch the numbers to determine how much money you must bring in every month to pay your bills and still make enough of a profit to maintain this space and make it worth your while.

A well-appointed, comfortable shop can make the work of upholstery much more fun. In your home, or down the road, take some time to create a workspace that's enjoyable to be in and fits your practical needs; you'll be more likely to want to spend time there working, creating, and earning money.

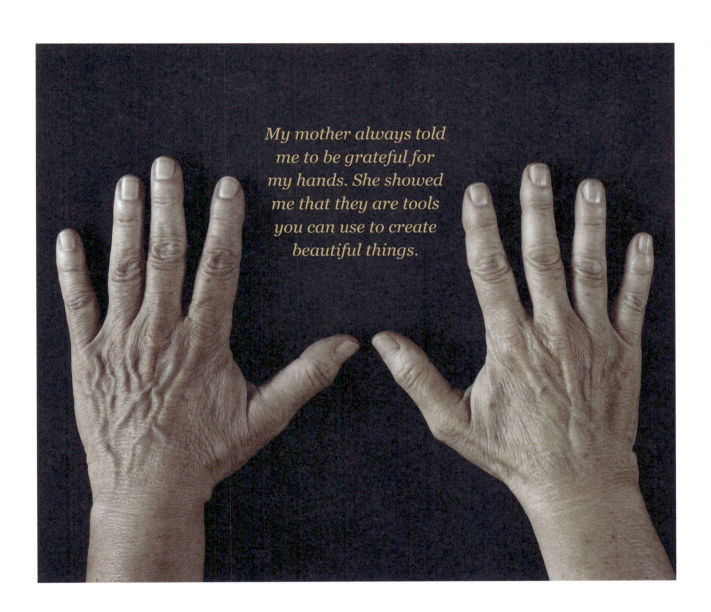

My mother always told me to be grateful for my hands. She showed me that they are tools you can use to create beautiful things.

Chapter Two

THE TOOLBOX

TOOLS

Before you get elbow-deep in coil springs, crumbly foam, and old cotton stuffing, you'll need to gather the right tools for the job. In the beginning, as you make your way through your first few pieces of furniture, it's wise to substitute common household tools you already have on hand. If and when you've committed to learning this craft, then you can treat yourself to authentic upholsterer's tools.

Where to Find Old Tools

Be on the lookout for upholsterers who are closing their shops and need to sell everything. Craigslist, eBay, or auctions are other good sources where an entire shop of tools and equipment can be purchased for very little. It's great fun, as well as educational, to go through an old-timey upholstery shop to investigate the eclectic collection of contents. Old tools and equipment usually work just as well, if not better, than new.

One of the first things that charms the eager new upholstery student is the look and feel of bona fide upholstery tools. The wood handles are designed to fit comfortably in the hands of skilled upholsterers, who spend eight hours a day "on the bench."

One reason I love upholstery tools of the trade is that they've changed very little over the past four hundred years. The original designs still perform their intended functions very well, they feel good in your hands, and they have quite a pleasant visual aesthetic. Other upholstery hand tool designs have come and gone, and some have found their way into upholsterers' toolboxes around the globe, but the good old original designs are the top choice of traditional, as well as modern, upholsterers.

The following list of tools will get you started with beginner-level projects. If you're in a bind and don't have just the right tool, don't worry. Clever upholsterers improvise with all kinds of tools and handmade gadgets to get the job done. As you build your skills and your pieces require more specialized or detailed work, there are a wide variety of specific tools you can add to your toolbox. Your tools will be an ever-growing and evolving collection.

Beginner's Tool Box

Safety glasses:

Always wear safety glasses when using power tools, pulling staples or tacks, and hammering. Little bits and pieces of wood and staples can break off and fly through the air. PROTECT YOUR EYES!

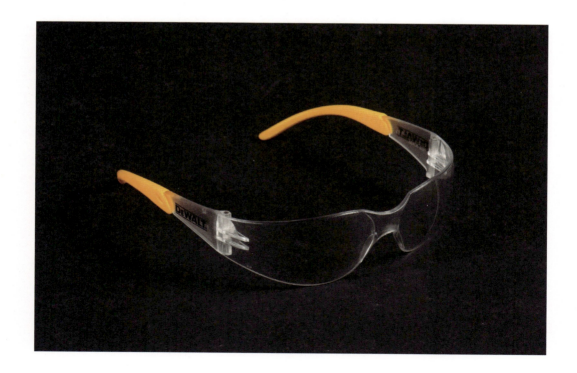

Staple lifters:

An upholstery-specific staple lifter or a flathead screwdriver is an essential tool to lift staples or tacks from furniture so you can remove old fabric and padding. Here are two kinds of specific staple lifters, as well as a small flathead screwdriver.

Pincers or pliers:

Hardware store crescent pliers are more than adequate to pinch and pull staples and tacks from wood frames. The pincer handles are ergonomically designed, and there are sharp snipper blades to clip stubborn staples.

Web stretcher:

There is just no substitute for a web stretcher. Both styles, gooseneck and straight, are designed to grab and hold webbing while you leverage the tool and pull the webbing taut over chair rails. Once it's stretched, the webbing is stapled (or tacked) onto the frame.

Hammer:

A small hammer will do just fine as a substitute for an upholsterer's tack hammer. The upholstery-specific hammer has magnetic ends for tacks or decorative nail heads. You can purchase a tack hammer with a nylon tip so as not to damage decorative nail heads as you're pounding them in place.

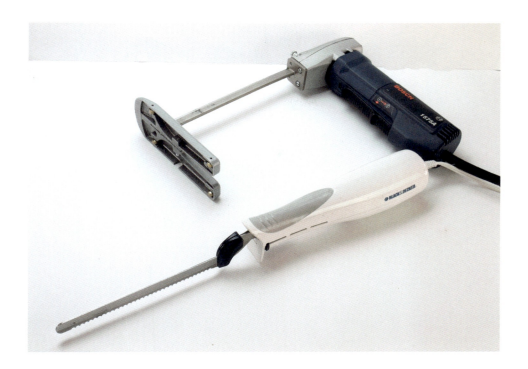

Electric knife or foam cutter:

When it's time to cut, sculpt, or contour foam, you'll need an electric bread knife or an upholsterer's foam cutter. The bread knife is reasonably priced at around $15.00, while this upholsterer's foam cutter retails for more than $400.00.

Shears:

Big, sharp scissors are a must when cutting upholstery fabric. It's also helpful to have a sharp pair of tiny scissors by your side during upholstery projects. Finally, a sharp utility knife comes in handy when cutting excess fabric away from a wood frame.

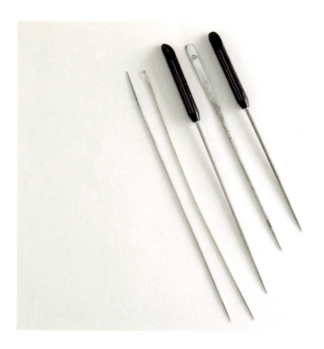

Upholstery regulator:

An upholstery regulator is used to move, arrange, and shift padding underneath fabric. It's also a handy tool to use when forming clean, sharp pleats and folds. You can substitute a long tufting needle or an ice pick.

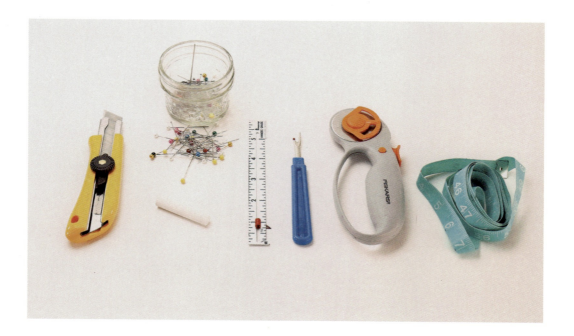

Marking tools:

Any kind of measuring, marking, and pinning supplies will suffice when you get ready to plan out and make your fabric cuts. I prefer chalkboard chalk, pencils, and straight pins for fabric marking, and fine felt-tip markers when tracing foam dimensions.

Needles:

An assortment of curved sewing needles, as well as straight tufting needles, are relatively inexpensive and are a must in your toolbox.

Staple guns:

The gun on the far left is a BeA long-nose pneumatic stapler. It's the best staple gun I've ever owned. Next to that is Orangey. She's pneumatic and has all-metal parts. She's been with me through thick and thin, and I hope she never dies. The next gun is probably the best buy for the beginner. It's budget friendly and available at Harbor Freight. It uses larger staples than an upholsterer's staple gun but, like Orangey, is powered by an air compressor. Once you try a pneumatic stapler, you'll never go back. And then there's Black Beauty, an electric stapler made by Maestri. I use it in all of my beginning classes.

Button maker:

This handy and simple button maker can be used to cover buttons with fabric or leather and set snaps, grommets, or ventilators. Variously sized 2 piece die sets and cutters are available. The button maker can be attached to a workbench for stability.

INDUSTRIAL SEWING MACHINE

If you're serious about learning upholstery, you'll need to learn how to sew. One of the first things you should invest in is either a heavy-duty home machine with a walking foot or an industrial upholstery-specific sewing machine. Finding a good one is easier said than done. If you're patient and keep your eyes peeled, you'll eventually come across a beefy home machine with all metal parts that's able to handle many layers of medium-weight to heavyweight fabric.

Sewing machines come in many shapes, colors, and designs, but the kind of machine you'll need for sewing home furnishings is no-nonsense, strong, and straightforward.

Sewing Machine Checklist

Straight stitch
Reverse stitch
Metal parts
Zigzag stitch (optional)
Nice, even stitches
Regular, zipper, and cording feet
Built-in walking foot (This is a must when sewing heavy fabrics. The mechanized center foot helps pull the top fabric under and through the machine at the same rate that the feed dog pulls the bottom fabric under the needle.)

Sewing machine feet:

A zipper foot can be used on your sewing machine to make fabric-covered welt cord. Most household machines come with a zipper foot. However, the industrial cording foot (*on the right*) has a hollowed-out arch in the bottom to allow the cording to quickly and smoothly feed under the presser foot. Double-welt-cord sewing machine feet are available for industrial upholstery sewing machines, and some home machines. If you can find cording feet for your machine, buy them. They make the job so much easier.

MORE SHOP TOOLS

Rubber mallet
Yardsticks and measuring tapes
Hot-glue gun
Iron and ironing board
Razor or box knife
Chalk and markers
Dressmaker pins and T-pins
Upholstery skewers
Hole saw or drill bit for cutting tufting holes
Air compressor
Channel tins for stuffing channel back chairs
Manual stapler
Brown or white paper for patternmaking
Drill and bits
Jigsaw

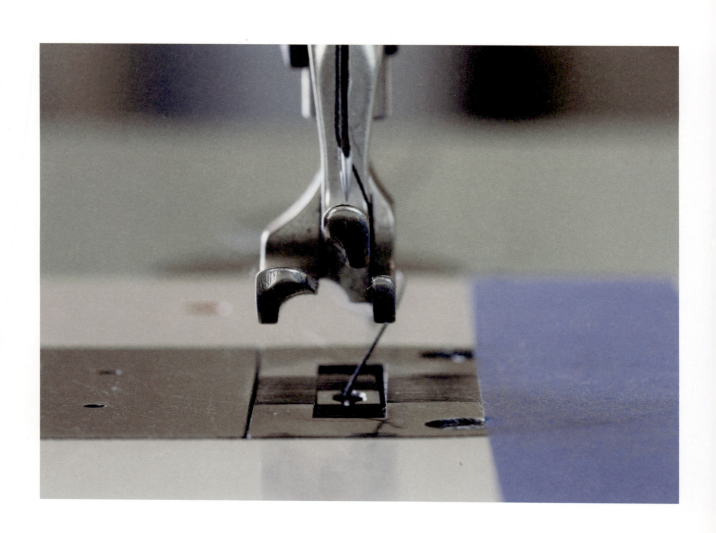

Chapter Three

THE MATERIALS AND SUPPLIES

I have always appreciated those who dare to experiment with materials and properties.

—Zaha Hadid, Iraqi British architect

Upholstery materials are tactile delights. Handling twine, webbing, burlap, and padding must be the reason why some of us can't kick the upholstery habit. "Materials and supplies," as used here, refers to consumable materials that go into a piece of furniture. From steel springs and tough jute webbing to soft cotton calico fabric, as well as steel wool, sandpaper, and first-aid supplies, these are items that get used up in an upholstery shop. You won't include things such as steel wool and first-aid supplies in your cost itemization for a piece of furniture, but they will be considered in your overhead costs.

Before you begin a work session, gather all the materials you'll need and set them out in a logical order. This keeps your workflow moving forward efficiently and keeps you from having to stop and fetch materials once you get a good rhythm to your work.

It's imperative that you keep a running tally of all materials that go into each piece. You'll need these numbers for inventory purposes, as well as custom pricing. Most modern-day upholsterers keep track of costs with an electronic bookkeeping system. I use QuickBooks for Business, but you'll need to find a system that works for you. This is your business—it needs to fit your style.

The list of consumable upholstery supplies can go on and on, but for the beginning-level projects in this book, the materials are basic to most upholstery shops. As your projects become more detailed or unusual, there are additional materials you may need. However, these will get you started.

Jute webbing is a staple of all upholstery shops. Its purpose is to provide a strong foundation for other materials that will be added in the upholstery process. Webbing can also be made from elasticized or synthetic fabric.

Cotton batting is used as padding. It can be used to insulate springs, act as a barrier layer between burlap and foam, serve as the padding on a simple slip seat, or fill in areas that need extra stuffing.

An upholstery shop needs lots of twine. From left to right, there's plain hemp twine, jute twine (spring tying), nylon tufting twine, and upholsterer's hand-sewing twine.

Upholstery tacks come in many sizes for many different uses. They still serve some purposes in modern upholstery but have been replaced, for the most part, by staples.

Traditional upholsterers still use tacks in their work. Old-timey upholsterers used to "spit tacks" by loading one side of their mouth with a number of tacks, skillfully rolling their tongue to pick up a tack on the magnetic end of their tack hammer, then pounding it in. They developed a rhythm that enabled them to work quickly and precisely.

Not all upholstery staples are alike. They come in different crown widths, different lengths, and different gauges. From left to right, $5/8$", $3/8$", and $1/4$" are the sizes most used.

Jute twine is used for spring tying. Coil springs, as well as sinuous springs, need to be secured to the chair frame as well as tied to each other to create optimum cushion with unified movement.

Cardboard tack strip is used to create a finished, straight edge. Fabric is flipped over, wrong side up, and staples are attached at a diagonal approximately $1/4"$ apart. The edge of the cardboard on the fold line creates a crisp edge.

Coil springs are used to provide comfort and support. They're affixed to a lower layer of woven jute webbing by stitching or clipping in place. Regardless of the piece of furniture, the springs are skillfully tied together to create a unified surface. Spring tying can get very fancy.

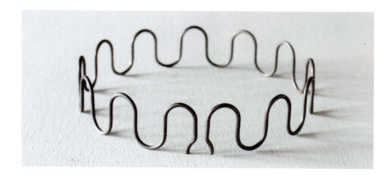

Sinuous, or zigzag, springs were invented to be installed on a chair frame with clips that are nailed to the seat rails and sometimes on the inside back rails. They create a crowned surface for subsequent padding. They also must be tied together and attached to the adjacent rails.

Burlap is used as a foundation fabric to cover springs and fill in open spaces in a piece of furniture.

Edge roll is often used on the top of seat rails. It used to be used to hold in loose padding materials, as well as to cushion the back of the legs when someone is seated. Older furniture usually has burlap-covered materials, but there's also a synthetic alternative.

Padding materials depend on a variety of factors. On the left are polyurethane foam and polyester Dacron. On the right is vegetable fiber for rough stuffing, in the center is soft horsehair filling, and at the bottom is cotton batting.

From left to right: spray adhesive for foam and other uses, dry-cleaning fluid for unexpected spotting as well as cleaning sticky hands, and silicone spray, used for lubricating foam cutter blades.

Nylon sewing machine thread comes in all colors and is strong enough for upholstery purposes.

A $^5/_{32}$" tissue-covered welt cord is the most common size for furniture and cushion welt cording. Rolls of double cording are also available from a supplier.

A roll of zipper tape enables the industrious upholsterer to create her own length of zippers depending on the job. Purchasing in bulk saves money.

Button shells come in all different sizes. Collect a good supply of sizes and backs for different purposes.

Cambric, an upholstery-specific, fused synthetic material, needs to be attached to the bottom of all finished pieces of furniture. However, any plain, lightweight fabric can be substituted for cambric. Cutting a piece $3/4"$ larger all around than the bottom of the frame, folding under halfway across the bottom rail, and stapling in place is all that is required.

There are any number of other materials you'll collect in you shop. Here are a few more that aren't pictured:

Decorative nailheads
Hot-glue sticks
Cotton muslin fabric
Canvas utility fabric
Assorted furniture hardware
Sandpaper
Steel wool
Clean rags
First-aid kit

Nickels and Dimes Count

The random materials that are routinely used in a shop may seem like a small cost, but every little thing you use adds up. These costs include thread, staples, hot glue, hardware, wood fillers, paint, furniture stain, wax, gliders, etc. They cost money, they get used up, and they have to be taken into consideration for bookkeeping purposes. You'll need to estimate how much of these you use in each project.

Sales Tax

If you do register in your state and receive a license to purchase materials with a tax-exempt status, you must keep copious records of your purchases in order to reconcile the state sales tax you'll owe at the end of a given period of time. It's the upholsterer's responsibility to keep track of the sales tax charged to each customer for the materials purchased and used in their product(s).

In my state, sales tax isn't charged on labor, but it is charged on the materials that go into a piece and that have been purchased with a tax-exempt status from your supplier. Check with your accountant to determine which materials are taxable so that you can accurately charge your customers.

Custom refurbished and reupholstered settee by Denver based Timber and Cloth.

If you start selling your own finished designs to retail customers through your shop or at art fairs or flea markets, as an end-product seller you are required to collect and pay sales tax to your state department of revenue on the total sale price of the finished piece. You can price your retail pieces so that tax is collected on top of your retail price—however, it can sometimes be easier, when you're selling at pop-up venues, to charge the retail customer an even amount. Then, take out the sales tax from the price charged and set that money aside to pay the collected sales tax when it's due. It may be monthly, quarterly, or annually. When you receive your retail merchant's license, you'll receive directions on how to file and pay your sales tax. Before you begin charging for your services or selling retail, consult with an accountant about your bookkeeping and sales tax obligations.

The supplier I've been using for over twenty years has recently substituted an inferior 60" wide roll of very thin and weak Dacron wrap for what was always a nice, strong-bonded Dacron wrap that was robust enough to split in two and get twice the use out of. I made a call to the office to let them know about the inferior product. Oftentimes, you'll end up with something unusable and need to bring it to the attention of your supplier right away. If they don't improve their products, you'll want to find a new supplier.

The maker movement is about people who want to gain more control of the human design world that they interact with every day. Instead of accepting off-the-shelf solutions from institutions and corporations, makers would like to make, modify, and repair their own tools, clothing, food, toys, furniture, and other physical objects.

—Mark Frauenfelder

section two

Timbers and Textiles

Chapter Four

FRAME ASSESSMENT AND BASIC REPAIR

TEARDOWN

Teardown refers to the process of stripping off old materials on a piece of furniture. This can simply entail removing the top fabric, or it can mean taking the covering and padding all the way down to the bare frame, or rails. The process can be grueling, but the finished chair is only as good as the preparation work. After the old materials are removed from the frame, then you'll have a blank canvas upon which you can create a masterpiece.

In my classes, it often turns out that a student's chair doesn't need to have the springs or webbing replaced. In that case, we may tighten things up and then start from there. Sometimes, though, things are such a mess that there's nothing else to do but tear everything off and start fresh.

With experience, you'll soon be able to ascertain what should stay and what should go. I recommend that you keep every piece that you remove for future reference and patternmaking.

If the foundation, springs, and padding are in excellent shape, you may only need to add a fresh layer of cotton or Dacron before upholstering with fresh, new fabric. If you're doing a piece for a customer, be sure to discuss with her that you won't know the full extent of the job until you can "get under the covers" and see what work needs to be done. Provide them with a price for a complete teardown and reupholstery job. If they agree, they'll be pleasantly surprised if the job winds up being less than you quoted. Lots of communication with your customers prevents misunderstandings after it's too late.

Chaise settee and accessories designed and created by Jess
Payne and Julia Woodmore. www.jessandjules.co.uk

The teardown process is, hands down, the best way to learn how furniture is built, how different kinds of foundations are installed, how padding is created and fit to size, and how fabric is aligned, cut, clipped, and made to wrap around the frame and attach to the rails.

Take plenty of photos during every stage of teardown. They'll provide a valuable road map as to how the piece was upholstered. However, not every upholstery job you encounter will have been correctly done. Look, learn, and think about what you encounter. You'll quickly pick up on standard techniques used by upholstery professionals.

Teardown Essentials:

Staple and tack lifter
Pincers or pliers
Hammer
Ripping tool (optional)
Scissors
Razor knife
Protective gloves (optional)
Safety glasses
A dust mask for extreme pieces
Drop cloth
Bandages
Antiseptic ointment

You might be surprised to learn that there's a standard, logical order in which fabric should be "unhitched" and removed from a piece of furniture. More simply stated, there's a method to this madness. Depending on the style and construction of a piece, there are always exceptions to the general rule of thumb. The following is the standard sequence of stripping the fabric and padding off a furniture frame for a fully upholstered wingback chair, armchair, love seat, or sofa.

STEP 1:

 Flip furniture over on top of a sturdy work surface so that you can comfortably access the bottom dustcover and remove the staples and cover.

STEP 2:

Working in the direction of the wood grain, loosen, lift, and remove all staples around the bottom rails. Always push the tool away from you as you're lifting tacks or staples, so as not to slip and gouge your other hand.

Keep your other hand out of the way! After you lift a staple, grab hold of it with a pair of pincers and gently roll your wrist to pull the staple out without breaking it off. If the staple breaks, get ahold of the broken-off nub and pull it out. If you can't remove it, pound it flush into the wood, using a tack hammer.

BEWARE: Staple pieces can catch your skin and cause injury.

STEP 3:

To remove the fabric from a piece, start with the outside back at the side closures. Whether it's hand stitched or closed up by using a metal strip called Curve Ease, you'll need to release each side of the back piece and then remove the back piece at the top rail of the outside back.

Once the outside back is removed, there is much to learn by peeking inside the chair frame. Take time to see how the fabric was cut, clipped, pulled, and secured on the inside rails with staples or tacks. Again, take photos of everything. You never know what you'll need to refer to when you're putting this piece back together.

Standard order of teardown:

Dustcover
Bottom rails
Outside back
Outside arms
Outside wings (if applicable)
Inside back
Inside arms
Inside wings (wingback chair)
Front apron or "nose" (stitched to the decking)
Seat

As each piece of fabric is removed, use a marker or white chalk and label each piece so that you know exactly what it is.

OB: Outside back
ROA: Right outside arm
LOA: Left outside arm
ROW: Right outside wing
LOW: Left outside wing
RIA: Right inside arm
LIA: Left inside arm
RIW: Right inside wing
LIW: Left inside wing
IB: Inside back
FB: Front band
S: Seat
A or N: Front apron or nose
D: Decking

STEP 4:

Next, remove all layers of padding or stuffing, taking photos of where and how each piece was attached.

STEP 5:

If the webbing and springs will be replaced, take a photo of how the springs are arranged and attached to the webbing. Remove tacks or staples from the webbing straps on the seat rails and set the springs and webbing aside.

Caution: Do not remove large construction staples, nails, or screws. This could compromise the strength and stability of the furniture frame.

STEP 6:

Neatly stack all fabric and materials and designate which materials can be reused in the project. If they are dirty and dusty, all materials should be placed in a large bag until you need to refer to them.

STEP 7:

Go back over the chair frame and remove all remaining staples, staple pieces, tacks, threads, and pieces of torn fabric. You'll be glad that you stripped the chair completely and have a clean frame to upholster.

FRAME ASSESSMENT AND WOBBLY JOINTS

Before purchasing an existing piece of furniture or accepting a piece for commission work, assess the overall condition of the piece. The outside upholstery fabric will be the first clue as to what you'll encounter. Next, try it out. Take a seat. If the springs are dangling out the bottom, or if you fall right through the seat frame, it's likely the piece will need to be completely stripped down and reupholstered.

It's difficult, if not impossible, to thoroughly examine the frame until you get the piece completely torn down.

Here's a quick "wiggle and wobble" checklist to help you determine if this piece is worth the money and time you'll have to invest in the refurbishment process.

- Grab the back of the frame firmly and move it back and forth to see if you detect any wiggling in the back frame.
- Grab the arms and wiggle them to see if there's any wiggling where the arms connect to the back of the frame.
- Grab the front corners of the arms and move them back and forth to see if there's any give in the front joints.
- Pick up the chair to see if it's medium to heavy weight. If it's unusually light, it's probably made from a soft, inexpensive wood.
- Sit down on the furniture to see how it feels. If you sink way down or fall through, you know the seat will have to be rebuilt from the foundation up.
- Tip the piece upside down. If there's a dustcover, you may not be able to see anything, but if there's a tiny tear in the dustcover, peek inside. You'll be looking for two things. First, you'll be investigating the upholstery needs, but while you're at it, check to see if there's any visible broken or split wood, loose screws, broken dowels, etc. All these things need to be repaired. You won't be able to see the entire frame and what structural repairs are needed until the piece is completely torn down.

If you're convinced that the piece is worth the purchase price, estimated time in labor, and cost of materials, then it's time to move forward and get busy.

Standing naked in all its glory, it's time to address wood repair, tighten screws and joints, and apply wood filler. If you notice the frame is infested with woodworm, now is the time to apply treatment.

The more you know about wood types, furniture joinery, and overall construction of furniture frames, the better qualified you are to repair cracks, splits, or wobbles that jeopardize the integrity of your frame. Whether you can handle the woodwork yourself or you need to pay an expert to do the repairs, a solid, sturdy frame is the first step to successfully rehabbing a piece of furniture.

It's difficult to learn wood and furniture repair at the same time you're learning and practicing new upholstery skills. For the projects in this book, upholstery skills and strategy should be your primary focus.

Chapter Five

USER-FRIENDLY FABRICS AND HANDMADE TEXTILES

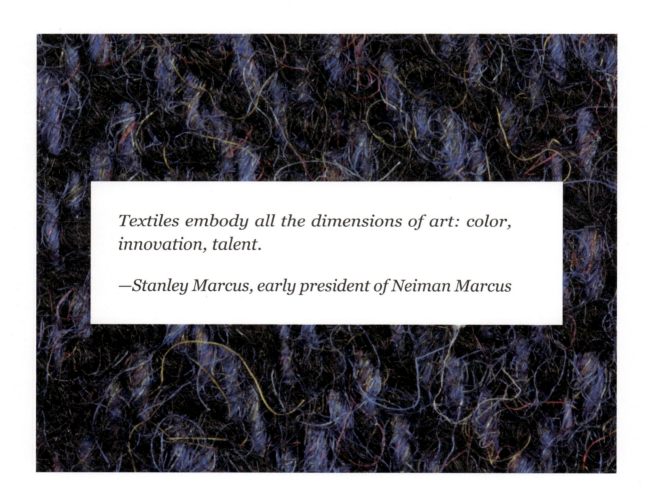

Textiles embody all the dimensions of art: color, innovation, talent.

—Stanley Marcus, early president of Neiman Marcus

It's a stroke of luck when you get to work with fabrics that excite you. It's not always possible to be thrilled when you're locked into your customer's fabric selection—however, as you gain experience and knowledge, you'll be able to confidently guide your customers in their choices. When you do enjoy working with a specific fabric, it makes the job all that much more fun and stress free, which is a benefit for learning basic upholstery skills.

In the beginning, as you're building skills and mastering techniques, it's helpful to be working with fabrics that allow you to focus on upholstery skills without getting bogged down in the challenges of using finicky or pattern-challenging fabrics. If you concentrate on honing your skills first, you'll have plenty of time for fabric experimentation later; now is the time to focus on skills and techniques.

FABRIC CONSIDERATIONS

In order to choose an appropriate and pleasing fabric for a piece of furniture, you need to understand a few interior design basics regarding upholstery fabric.

Pattern/scale: How the size of a pattern will look on the size of any given piece of furniture. For example, a large-scale print can overwhelm a small chair. On the other hand, a stunning piece of fabric can turn an average chair into an eye-popping showstopper.

Pink Opal chair redesigned and traditionally upholstered by Andrea Mihalik, owner of Wild Chairy, Philadelphia, Pennsylvania.

Color: Some experts think that bold colors should be used on smaller pieces, while more-neutral fabrics should reside on larger pieces. Colors can determine the entire mood of a space.

Fiber content: The fiber content of fabrics affects their draping ability, durability, folding, stitching, snagging, puckering, pulling, and unwanted tearing. Content matters.

Upholstery fabrics, like apparel fabrics, are woven with fibers. Fibers can fall into one of three categories: natural, synthetic, or a blend of both.

    Natural: Cotton, silk, wool, and linen.

    Synthetic: Acetate, acrylic, nylon, polyester, and rayon.

    Blended: Fabrics that are woven with natural and synthetic fibers of differing percentages.

    All natural fabrics have their drawbacks when used in upholstery, as do all synthetic fabrics. However, an upholstery fabric that's a blend of natural and synthetic fibers can make up a lovely and durable fabric appropriate for upholstering. When the blend is done right, you get the benefits of both: the beauty of natural fibers combined with the durability of synthetic fibers.

Durability: How well a fabric holds up over time with general wear and tear is determined by the fibers that combine to create the fabric.

Cleaning: 100 percent natural fabrics such as cotton, linen, and wool can be difficult, if not impossible, to clean. Synthetic blends are easier to clean. The jury's still out on whether fabric treatments make fabrics substantially easier to clean and more stain resistant. Most fabrics come from the mill with a fabric treatment.

Hand: The overall feel of a fabric in your hands will likely be consistent with how it looks and behaves while upholstering. If it feels too thin, it will be difficult to tug, pull into place, secure with staples, and have staples removed from it, if necessary. It just won't hold up. A fabric that feels too thick or stiff in your hands is difficult to manipulate when folding and tucking in corners and edges.

Weave: The weave of fabrics largely determines how easy they'll be to use for upholstery, especially for the new upholsterer. Weave also affects stain resistance and durability over time. There are three main weaves of fabric: plain, twill, and satin. Within each category, there are variations that offer other benefits of appearance and function.

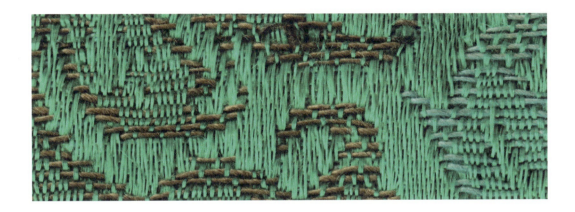

Fabric designs and patterns are generally either screen printed on the surface of a plain weave or twill fabric or woven into more-complex fabrics. As you upholster more and more pieces of furniture, you'll be gaining valuable fabric education and will understand the strengths and weaknesses of many fabrics.

"The jacquard weave is created by using an attachment known as the Jacquard Attachment. It allows for the weaving of fabric with curves, swirls, and large-sized figures."
 —Bernard P. Corbman in *Textiles: Fiber to Fabric* (New York: McGraw-Hill, 1975)

HANDMADE TEXTILES

Handmade textiles are front and center right now, and it's doubtful that they're going away any time soon. Used mostly for light furnishings, the current interest in reupholstering furniture with handmade textiles allows furniture to become functional art that will command higher prices due to its one-of-a-kind status. There's often a higher-end market for well-made vintage pieces upholstered with handmade textiles. People love to own one-of-a-kind pieces.

"One of a kind" is a market in which you can create smaller pieces of upholstered furniture and turn a quick profit if you know who your customer is, how to market to them, and how to sell them your designs.

It's not necessary to travel to exotic locations to pick up interesting pieces of suitable textiles, although it can be fun and exciting to search the world for unique goods.

Nowadays, you can also easily create your own handmade textiles by using techniques such as *shibori*, block printing, appliqué, quilting, and more. Upholstered furniture art is attracting an ever-increasing number of artists and artisans who are pushing the envelope by exploring the medium through fabrics, finishes, and clever detail techniques. Many artists have already become established through using furniture as their canvas and securing their own gallery shows, as well as building a curious fan base. Curated-furniture shows are a way to showcase individual styles and talents. If there are no opportunities in your area, organize you own show and invite others to join you.

Chair redesign by fabric artist, upholsterer, teacher Maaike Pullar, Sydney, Australia.

FABRIC TERMINOLOGY

Bias: The exact 45° (diagonal) direction of the fabrics. Cutting fabric on this angle cuts through both the vertical and horizontal threads, allowing the cut edge to have more stretch.

Double rub: A test that's conducted to attest to the durability of the fabric by using a mechanical device to repetitively rub across the surface of a fabric. The double-rub number indicates how many back-and-forth rubs it takes for the fabric to show abrasion.

Fade resistance: How vulnerable a fabric design is to fading over time.

Fibers: The natural or man-made material that is twisted together to form threads.

Grain: The vertical and horizontal threads that create fabric.

Nap: A fabric that has cut fiber ends sticking out from the fabric base. Velvets, chenilles, corduroys, and microfibers are examples.

Pattern: The design that's either woven into the fabric through the weave or printed onto the fabric surface.

Railroaded: Fabric usually runs down the bolt from top to bottom, whether it's a design or fabric nap. Fabric is considered railroaded when it is printed or woven with the design running lengthwise down a fabric roll with the selvages (*see below*) on the top and bottom of the usable fabric design. Railroading allows upholsterers to cover chairs, love seats, or sofas in widths greater than 54" without having to stitch fabric widths together.

Repeat: The measurement between repeated designs either woven in or printed on the surface of fabric. The repeat is measured from the top of one motif to the top of the next repeated motif.

Selvage: The two tightly woven edges of fabric yardage where the threads were attached to the loom. It usually includes the manufacturer and a color guide.

Weave: The method in which the vertical and horizontal threads are woven together to form cloth.

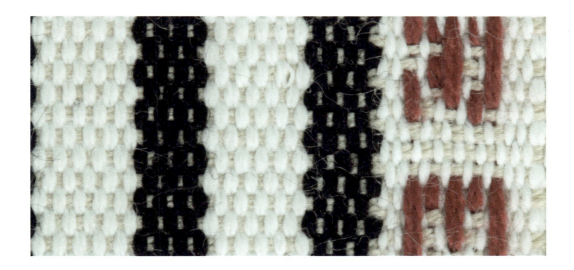

There's always a top and bottom to fabric yardage, but sometimes it's nearly undetectable. When there's a nap to a fabric such as velvet, or a directional motif, such as a vase of flowers, the new pieces need to be laid out as if the fabric is running down the piece of the furniture from top to bottom.

With a napped fabric, the fibers should lie flat from top to bottom. When you run your hands over the nap, one direction will be smooth while the other direction will feel rougher.

ESTIMATING FABRIC YARDAGE

The quickest way to determine how much fabric you'll need for a project is to look at a fabric yardage estimation chart. This basic cheat sheet has been around for decades.

You simply find the picture of the piece of furniture that looks most similar to the one you're upholstering, and then see what the recommended fabric yardage is. I usually add an extra half yard to be on the safe side. There are some other factors to consider before you hastily accept the recommended yardage on the chart.

If you have a fabric pattern with a noticeable repeat (larger than 3"), you'll need to increase the total yardage in order to accommodate the pattern matching you'll have to do. The larger the repeat, the more fabric you'll need. *Repeat* means how many inches there are from the beginning of one pattern to the beginning of the next.

Sailrite Fabric Yardage Chart

Figures represent the approximate amount of yardage needed for 54" wide material.

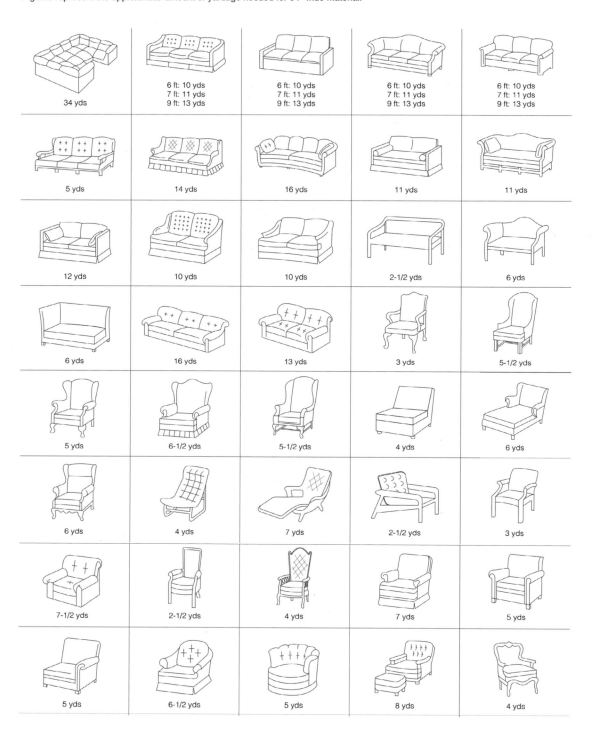

34 yds	6 ft: 10 yds 7 ft: 11 yds 9 ft: 13 yds	6 ft: 10 yds 7 ft: 11 yds 9 ft: 13 yds	6 ft: 10 yds 7 ft: 11 yds 9 ft: 13 yds	6 ft: 10 yds 7 ft: 11 yds 9 ft: 13 yds
5 yds	14 yds	16 yds	11 yds	11 yds
12 yds	10 yds	10 yds	2-1/2 yds	6 yds
6 yds	16 yds	13 yds	3 yds	5-1/2 yds
5 yds	6-1/2 yds	5-1/2 yds	4 yds	6 yds
6 yds	4 yds	7 yds	2-1/2 yds	3 yds
7-1/2 yds	2-1/2 yds	4 yds	7 yds	5 yds
5 yds	6-1/2 yds	5 yds	8 yds	4 yds

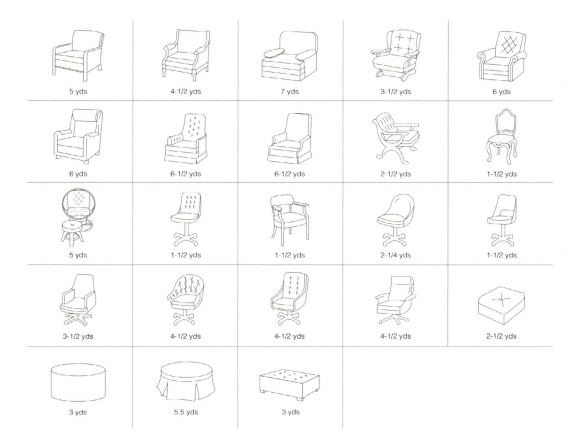

5 yds	4-1/2 yds	7 yds	3-1/2 yds	6 yds
6 yds	6-1/2 yds	6-1/2 yds	2-1/2 yds	1-1/2 yds
5 yds	1-1/2 yds	1-1/2 yds	2-1/4 yds	1-1/2 yds
3-1/2 yds	4-1/2 yds	4-1/2 yds	4-1/2 yds	2-1/2 yds
3 yds	5.5 yds	3 yds		

(800) 348-2769 / (260) 244-4647 / Sailrite.com

As a savvy new upholsterer, you'll want to be able to look at any given piece of furniture and calculate how much fabric you'll need to get the job done without skimping. This has to accurately reflect pattern matching and any other layout requirements.

In upholstery, you need to discover what works best for you time and time again. Many veteran upholsterers advise measuring everything down to absolute exact micromillimeters in order to determine the best and most efficient use of fabric yardage. That's good advice and perfectly acceptable, but it's not the only way to estimate and determine fabric needs. Some people may need exact measurements, while others might feel perfectly comfortable and confident using their intuitive abilities to come up with the necessary yardage for any given piece. Again, you need to find the methods that work for you and still fall within the spectrum of accepted upholstery standards.

PRO TIP: Standard 54"-wide upholstery fabric is measured from outside edge to outside edge of the selvages. That means that within a cut width of fabric, there is at least one inch of unusable material.

I recommend cutting off the selvages before you get started. For one thing, they tend to be more tightly woven and can pucker. Second, you don't want even the slightest bit of selvage to be seen on a finished piece of upholstered furniture, unless it's used intentionally as a design element.

Rough Estimating

Often, people casually ask me how much fabric is needed for a piece of furniture they're considering for reupholstery. In order to come up with a rough estimate on the fly, without measuring or referring to the chart, I simply do this:

I look at the piece head-on and think of each piece of fabric as being a big piece of paper attached to a padded surface.

One yard will typically be a piece of fabric 54" wide by 36" long. I add up how many of those yards or half yards it will take to cover the chair. I then add 0.5 yard to 1 yard of extra fabric for a nonrepeat fabric and tell the customers they'll need more if they choose a fabric with a medium- to large-scale repeat. This provides potential customers with a ballpark idea of what they're looking at in terms of fabric needs. If they decide to reupholster the piece, I require them to choose their fabric so that we know whether there is a repeat to consider, and then I can provide them with a precise fabric estimate before they make their purchase.

Pattern Layout

With an iron temperature that won't melt your fabric, press each old pattern piece so that it lies flat on top of the new fabric. Make sure each piece has been marked with its proper location.

S: Seat
IB: Inside back
D: Seat deck
FB: Front band (attached to seat deck)
C: Cushion pieces: top, bottom, band (also known as boxing)
Z: Zipper band (with zipper installed)
RIA: Right inside arm
LIA: Left inside arm
RIW: Right inside wing
LIW: Left inside wing
ROW: Right outside wing
LOW: Left outside wing
ROA: Right outside arm
LOA: Left outside arm
OB: Outside back
Also, designate the top of each piece of fabric.

BIZ TIP: The old fabric pieces that come off a piece should not be considered perfect pattern pieces for your newly repadded piece of furniture. The pieces you removed have been used, stretched, twisted, distorted, and trimmed. They're good guides, but you should always take measurements for each section after adding new materials and padding before you cut them out. If you use them as an exact pattern, you'll be heartbroken when there's not enough fabric to grab hold and get a good and taut pull so that it can be secured to the frame. Write down the measurements for each piece and add at least 2"–4" all around.

Once you've purchased your fabric yardage, you'll want to make the best use of each and every inch. For my learning style, the most helpful way to understand fabric layout and the arrangement of pieces was to unroll the fabric and lay out all the pattern pieces. It's easy to move the pieces around, visualize, and measure out how the pieces will be cut out of the new fabric.

Determine which end is the designated "top" of your fabric. Mark it with chalk or a pin. Every fabric has a top edge, even though it can be nearly impossible to discern. Usually, the top of the fabric yardage is the cut edge that comes off the roll, unless it's railroaded.

Place your labeled and pressed pieces on the new fabric so that you have an idea of how each piece will fit. Take into account the new measurements due to fresh padding, as well as the extra 2" around each piece.

If your fabric has a repeat larger than 3", this real layout exercise will enable you to plan the design repeats on the furniture as you want them to be.

Move the pattern pieces around to find the optimal use of fabric.

Once you've laid out all of the pieces, review them again before cutting.

You can never measure too many times. I like to take it one piece at a time, but some upholsterers would rather cut everything out all at once.

Fabric-Covered Welt Cord

Using 54" wide fabric that is cut on the bias and $5/32$" cord:

- 1 yard of fabric cut into $1^3/_4$" bias strips will produce 26 yards of fabric-covered welt cord.
- 1 yard of fabric cut into $2^1/_2$" bias strips will produce 18 yards of double-welt cord.

Welt cord can also be made out of fabric strips cut on the straight grain of the fabric—however, they're limited in how much stretch they have for curves and turning corners.

REMEMBER:

Even the best upholsterers can run up against fabrics that are difficult to use for some reason or another. This can present a welcome challenge on a good day but can cause unplanned delays when working within a tight time frame. Patience and perseverance always pay off.

section three

Skill Building

Chapter Six

THE PROJECTS

One of the greatest and simplest tools for learning more and growing is doing more.

—Washington Irving

The majority of new upholstery students who come into our workshops are under the mistaken impression that learning how to upholster like a pro is an easy feat that won't take longer than six or seven weeks. They quickly discover that it takes more practice and patience than they imagined. It's a skill that is acquired over time with lots of practice, lots of mistakes, and lots of successes. The most effective way to learn upholstery is to approach this craft with a beginner's mind and expect to make mistakes that will teach you valuable lessons.

Professional upholsterers have many time-saving tips and techniques that make the demanding work of upholstering more efficient and streamlined. The sooner the new upholstery student embraces and practices proper techniques, the sooner those new skills can be applied to a myriad of projects that will generate revenue for her.

When I was starting out in the business, I had taken two live courses at a local vocational school and had one book in hand to use as a guide. Although I had years of sewing and "making" experience, it was necessary for me to put aside my preconceptions and accept the methods being taught by people who knew more than I did.

There are many right ways to upholster a piece of furniture, but there are also many wrong ways. Learn one of the right ways and you'll never be sorry.

Before embarking on this empowering and exciting journey, take a moment to honor the years of training and experience it takes to become a proficient and professional upholsterer. You'll soon appreciate how much dedication it takes to truly master this craft. An experienced teacher of upholstery may simply not be available in the near future.

THE PROJECTS

Buttoned-Down Blue Velvet Footstool
Perfect Kitchen Chair Do-Over
Leather-Trimmed Valet Bench Remodel
Low-Slung Midcentury Modern Lounger
Rockin' Moroccan Hanging Headboard

The projects in this book have been mindfully designed and organized for the upholstery beginner to build basic skills, learn techniques, and gain confidence for progressively taking on more-complicated pieces. The most-often-heard piece of advice from my students is "start small!" With that in mind, let's get started.

Now it's time to gather your tools and start building your skills.

The basic tools you need by your side don't change much from project to project. Here's a list of what you'll always want at your workbench, or within arm's reach.

Staple lifter
Pincers or crescent pliers
Tack hammer
Regulator
Scissors
Curved needles
Tufting needles
Staple gun
Straight edges
Measuring tape
Black marker
Pencil
White school chalk
Electric knife
Web stretcher
Drill with bits
Phillips and flathead screwdrivers
Sandpaper and small electric sander

***If a specialty tool is necessary, the tool will be specified under each project introduction.

I look at every piece of furniture and every object as an individual sculpture.

—Kelly Wearstler

Project 1:

BUTTONED-DOWN
BLUE VELVET FOOTSTOOL

When wandering around flea markets, estate sales, or antique malls, keep your eyes peeled for solid little vintage footstools with some unusual element. If they're new and inexpensive, they may not possess anything special that translates into value. Learn everything you can about what makes furniture attractive, of value, and unique. Your upholstery know-how, furniture knowledge, and overall expertise in the vintage furniture marketplace will win customer loyalty.

Old vintage stools with unique legs and hardwood frames are easy to repair and transform into highly desirable accent pieces when reupholstered using a trendy fabric, one-of-a-kind textile, unique legs, or some other special design element.

This little beat-up stool has seen better days. However, it was purchased for next to nothing at an architectural salvage yard here in my city. The owners thought they were getting a good deal when I paid them $5 for it (the legs alone are worth at least $20). Once it's repaired, repadded, and reupholstered, it will be a gem of an accent piece that will add a touch of sophistication to any decorating style. The fact that this piece was transformed into a completely refurbished vintage piece adds an environmentally responsible aspect to the story of this precious find.

Skills

Wood repair and corner reinforcement
Corner block replacement and installation
T-nut installation
Web stretching
Burlap attachment
Measuring and cutting foam
Securing foam to burlap base
Dacron cutting and attachment
Fabric placement, measuring, and cutting
Tidy folded corners
Covered buttons and installation
Leg attachment
Dustcover

Materials and Supplies

Sawdust
Wood glue
Screws
T-nuts
Jute webbing
$3/8$" staples
Burlap
2" foam
Dacron batting or cotton batting
Fabric
Button molds (shells)
Tufting twine
Nylon sewing thread or upholsterer's hand-sewing thread
Black cambric for dustcover
4 furniture legs that will fit T-nuts

Special Tools

Button maker or button-making kit
Spatula for wood filling
Chop saw / miter saw
Electric sander (optional)

What You Do:

Step 1:

Strip off the old fabric.

Wood Repair and New Corner Block Installation

Step 2:

Remove the damaged corner blocks. Place 3 tablespoons of sawdust in a bowl. Mix in wood glue until you have a paste that looks like tuna salad. Fill all cracks and holes in the old frame by pressing the wood filler into them. Let it dry thoroughly.

Step 3:

 Smooth the dried glue with sandpaper or a small sander.

Step 4:

 Use the old corner blocks to trace and cut new corner blocks for installation.

Step 5:

 On a flat surface, place the new corner blocks snugly into each corner. While holding the block in place, drill two pilot holes for attaching the corner blocks to the stool frame. (Always use a drill bit slightly smaller than your wood screw diameter.)

Installing Furniture Leg T-nuts

T-nuts are nifty little threaded sleeves that have a flange on the top with four metal grips on the underside that embed in the wood to hold it in place when hammered into the drilled hole. The furniture leg bolts go up into the drilled corner block and grab on to the threaded bottom of the sleeve. When the legs are screwed in snugly, the flange with the metal grips gets pulled down into the wood so that the nut won't spin or move. In order to make room for the leg bolt and the T-nut, you'll need to use a drill bit slightly larger than the diameter of the T-nut threaded sleeve.

Step 6:

Measure where the new leg bolts will be installed in the corner blocks and mark those measurements on each block. Drill straight through each block. From the top of the stool frame, pound the T-nuts in place with a hammer until the flange is tightly against the surrounding wood. Attach all four legs. Make the necessary adjustments if the legs aren't stable. You can add washers up on top of the leg bolts for more height. Make any adjustments at this time, before the top of the stool is upholstered.

Web Stretching

Web stretching is a mandatory skill for any upholsterer. Knowing how to create a tightly woven jute web base is fundamental to most all upholstery projects. In seating, stretched webbing does the "heavy lifting" by bearing the weight of the forthcoming upholstery materials, but also the continual wear and tear of humans sitting down and getting up. For this reason, use the longest staples your stapler can handle.

Step 7:

Measure and mark the center of each rail on which you'll be attaching webbing. Keep the webbing on the roll and close to you as you begin by securing the cut end away from you. Beginning ³/₄" from the cut end, secure the webbing to the rail at the midpoint of the rail width. Attach the webbing with five staples across. Fold the remaining cut end over the row of staples and add three more staples to secure the end in place.

Step 8:

Now you're going to use the web stretcher as leverage to pull the webbing tight across the rails. Repeat step 7 by stapling, cutting, folding, and securing the cut ends down.

Step 9:

Complete the webbed base by alternating the weaving of the strips and attaching them to the rails according to the above steps.

Step 10:

Cut a piece of burlap that measures 1" larger all around than the outside measurements of the top rails of the stool. Example: for a stool measuring 12" x 14", you'll need a piece of burlap that measures 14" x 16". This allows enough burlap to pull snugly, staple, fold over, staple again, and trim.

Step 11:

Attach the first side of the burlap with 2–4 staples at the centers of each side of the stool, beginning at the center on the side closest to you. Move to the opposite side, and then the remaining two sides. Next, attach remaining burlap by moving out toward each corner, keeping the burlap straight and pulled snugly as it's stapled in place. This is the four-point stapling method.

Finally, starting in the center of each side, fold the cut burlap edge over itself and staple it down neatly. Trim excess, if needed.

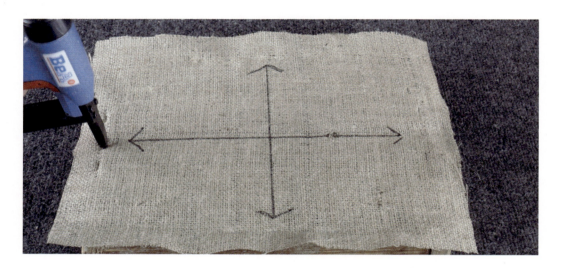

Foam Measuring and Cutting

Step 12:

Place the stool frame on top of 2" foam. Trace the outside of the stool frame, leaving $1/2$" extra all around. Use an electric knife or a foam cutter to cut the foam. Bevel the top edge of the foam at a 45° angle.

PRO TIP: Use silicone spray on the cutting blades to help them glide through the foam easily.

76

Step 13:

Spray adhesive on the burlap surface and the underside of the foam. Center and press foam firmly in place.

Step 14:

Measure, cut, and use adhesive to attach Dacron batting to the foam. Do not pull the Dacron underneath the side rails. It should stop flush with the bottom edges of each rail. Dacron doesn't have to be stapled in place but it can be, if needed. Trim off excess Dacron so that it's flush with the edges of the rails. Lastly, cut off the Dacron excess "triangles" from each corner.

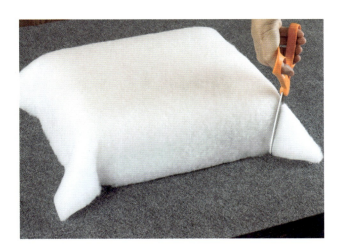

Step 15:

Measure the newly padded stool for upholstery fabric.

Always add 2–3 extra inches of fabric beyond where the fabric will ultimately be stapled to the rail. This allowance is known as "pull," and it provides enough fabric for leverage as you pull it snugly for stapling.

Step 16:

Place fabric on a flat cutting surface. Place the stool on the fabric, mark the cut lines with pins or chalk (that won't show), and cut out the stool upholstery fabric. Set aside.

Step 17:

Determine the placement for the covered buttons. Use long pins or tufting needles to try different arrangements. Once you know where you want the buttons, flip the stool over and mark the webbing where the buttons will be attached.

Upholstering

It's time to master the often-used technique for upholstering a square or rectangular frame that has been webbed and padded. You'll use this method for many different pieces of furniture. The four-point method ensures a smooth, taut top fabric that won't get saggy or baggy, if done correctly.

Step 18:

Measure and mark the center points of both of the long rails of the stool. Fold your cut fabric in half crosswise and clip a small "v" notch that will indicate the center of your fabric's front and back.

Step 19:

Starting in the center, smooth the fabric over the top edge and anchor the fabric on the center of the bottom of the rail with 3–4 staples.

Next, move to the opposite side and use your hand to firmly compress and smooth the fabric while stapling the fabric at the center of the bottom rail. Check the fabric grain to make sure it's still aligned vertically and horizontally.

Next, move to the centers of the short sides of the stool and repeat the process. Now all four sides should be pulled smooth and taut, with approximately 4" of fabric left unstapled on either side of each corner.

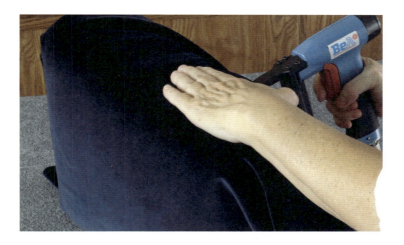

PRO TIP: The technique of smoothing and pulling the fabric out and at a diagonal toward the corners as you staple works to compress the foam while smoothing sharp top edges of foam-covered seating such as benches, dining-room chair seats, and ottomans. It also eliminates the ripple effect that occurs when you pull the fabric straight down on the grain and staple it in place. The diagonal pull is a valuable tool for smooth edges.

Step 20:

Prior to finessing the corners, place a piece of soft-spun Dacron up into each corner. The purpose is to have some filling available if you need to plump up the corner folds when you're finished—not causing lumps, but filling out puckers or loose fabric. If you don't need it, it's unobtrusive.

Creating the Perfect Folded Corners

Tight and tidy folded corners is the "must master" technique for any new upholsterer. Building your business by doing simple, foam-padded, wrapped seating and stools is an easy and profitable way to start generating income for your burgeoning skills. Here's how to get the professional corners that customers are willing to pay for.

Step 21:

The fabric should be loose 4" out from each corner. This will give you enough room to create the perfect fold.

Beginning with a corner on one short side of the stool, pull and smooth the fabric evenly around the corner with a slight pull diagonally downward, then anchor the pulled fabric with a staple just beyond the frame corner. Anticipate where the fabric will be folded on the corner edge.

About 1" inside that fold, cut out a square of excess fabric to eliminate the bulk. Pull snugly and staple the corner in place. Repeat for the other three corners.

Covered Buttons

You'll need to make fabric-covered buttons with an upholsterer's button-making tool. You can try using the button-making kits from the fabric store, but covered buttons made with a commercial button maker are more likely to hold up with everyday wear and tear. If you don't have a button maker, an upholstery shop is usually willing to make covered buttons for you for a minimal fee.

Button makers accept different-sized die parts for making different-sized covered buttons. For this project, we used size 36 button shells and backs.

Mini Workshop: Making Covered Buttons

Step 22:

There's a cutting die for each size of button. Cut out the proper-sized fabric circles for your buttons.

Place the button back into the base of the other piece of the button die, with the wire eye down.

To make a button, place one fabric circle on top of the button-making die, right side down.

Place a button shell on top of that piece of fabric and push the fabric and mold down into the die.

Place the loaded die on top of the bottom die and firmly pull the button maker handle down 2–3 times. Lift the die top and remove the covered button. Repeat for as many buttons as you need.

Step 23:

The easiest way to attach buttons is to cut a piece of 22" long tufting twine. Fold it in half and thread the fold through the eye of the button back. Take the two cut ends and thread them through the loop formed by the folded twine. Pull snug.

Step 24:

Re-establish the button placement on top of the final fabric. Thread one end of the twine through the eye of one long tufting needle. Pull it through and out through the webbing on the bottom side of the footstool. Thread the other cut end of the twine through the eye of the needle and, moving the needle to the right approximately $1/4$", thread the end of the twine through to the back of the stool. Repeat for all four buttons, making sure the placement is even. Next, using 3" of scrap webbing, roll it up tightly and tie the twine around the roll of webbing. Make sure all buttons are pulled down uniformly before knotting the twine. A slip knot can be used in order to make adjustments in the button depth prior to tying off each button.

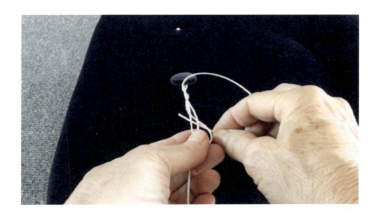

Wrapping Up

Step 25:

Measure, cut, and attach a piece of dustcover or cambric to the bottom of the footstool. The cambric is cut approximately ³/₄" larger all around so that the edges can be folded under and attached.

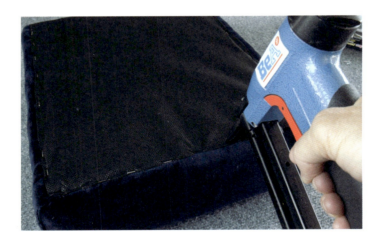

Step 26:

Use a needle to find the furniture leg holes, and poke small holes in the cambric to allow the leg bolts to be screwed into the bottom of the frame. Screw each leg snugly into the bottom of the stool. Since the cambric is a fused material, poking a hole in it will rarely cause any damage. Turn the stool upright to see if it needs adjusting. Sometimes adding a washer at the top of the leg bolt will even out an uneven leg (rubber washers work best).

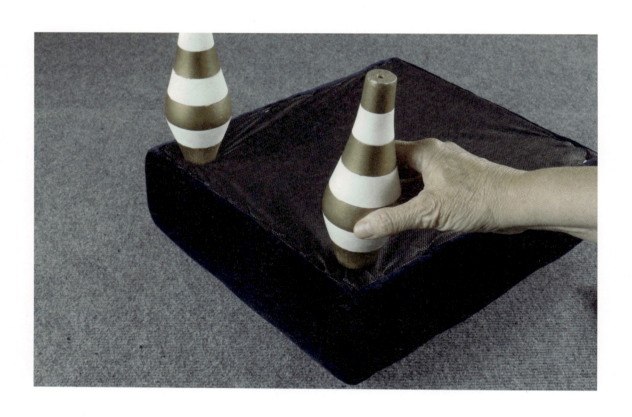

Project 2:

PERFECT KITCHEN CHAIR DO-OVER

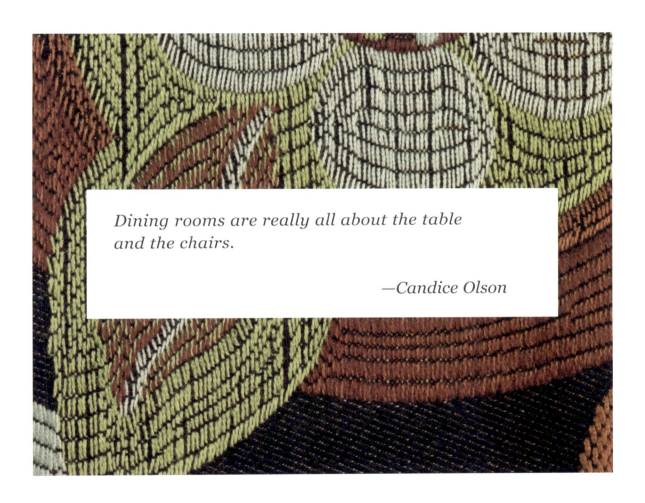

Dining rooms are really all about the table and the chairs.

—Candice Olson

Granted, it's tempting to dive into an upholstery job that's a wee bit beyond your current abilities. A much-better tack to take is to start with simple projects with which you can learn and execute your growing skills little by little, until you feel confident and proficient.

Most upholstery teachers require students to start their education by learning to completely reupholster a slip seat or wrapped seat. That's a simple seat base, foam, batting, and fabric wrapped and attached on the bottom of the base. Another reason to master this skill right away is that the jobs are readily available, and customers usually need four or more of these seats reupholstered at a time. It's an easy job that can yield a hefty profit, especially if you're lucky enough to get hired to do 8–10 chairs. Kitchen and dining chair seats will be a constant in your business. If you learn how to do them well, in a timely fashion and for a fair price, you'll have a robust cash cow service to boost your revenue.

This kitchen chair do-over is a notch above a basic wrapped seat in that it's a boxed seat cover with two fabric-covered panels for the inside back and outside back of the chair. The top of the seat is a cut piece of fabric that has a "boxing," or band, stitched around it that will cover the seat edges. Boxed seat coverings may have fabric-covered welt cording stitched between the seat top and the boxing. We chose not to include welt cord, or piping, in the seam of this high-end wool seat covering.

When you learn how to create a stitched boxed seat cushion attached to a wood base, you'll be ready to knock out kitchen chair seats, long bench seats, footstools, ottomans, daybeds, and more. The pattern repeat in this high-end fabric provides a beginner's lesson in pattern matching.

Easing, stitching, and stapling a fabric cover over a padded, slightly rounded wood base like this one necessitates slightly different fabric manipulation skills than a wood base with sharp corners. As your confidence grows, the better prepared you'll be to accept higher-paying jobs.

Skills

Fitting cotton batting over foam
Pattern matching on seat top and boxing
Pinning and stitching a boxed seat cover
Measuring, marking, and attaching a uniformly attached boxing
Easing, smoothing, and stapling fabric around curved corners
Upholstering thin wood panels
Invisibly attaching panels to the inside and outside back of a kitchen chair

Materials and Supplies

1" and 2" foam
Spray adhesive for foam (APC #79)
Cotton batting
Straight pins
Staples (1/4" and 3/8" long)
Black cambric or dustcover for bottom
Wood oil and clean rag

Special Tools

Seam ripper
Sewing machine

What You Do:

Step 1:

Strip the materials off the old seat and chair back panels. Clean up the chair frame with furniture cleaner and oil. Remove the old sewn fabric covering. Use a seam ripper to remove the boxing from the seat top. Press each piece flat to use as pattern pieces.

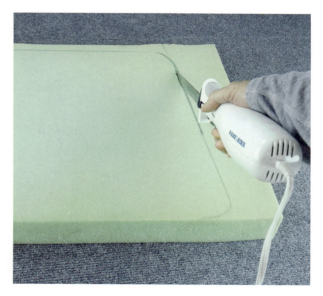

Step 2:

Remove the old foam and Dacron from the wood base. Place the wood base on top of a new piece of 2" foam and trace around the base. The new foam should be 1/2" larger all around than the wood base. Use a bread cutter or foam cutter to cut out the foam.

Step 3:

Use a strong foam adhesive (I use APC #79 foam adhesive) to adhere the foam to the wood seat base.

Step 4:

Instead of using Dacron batting, we're going to use cotton batting for the soft layer on top of the foam. Smooth it over the top of the seat and sides. To remove the excess batting, gently "feather" it out to the bottom edge of the foam. Do not cut cotton batting with scissors.

Step 5:

Use the old seat top as a pattern to cut out the new fabric. The top piece should be cut identically to the pattern piece, since it has to be stitched to the boxing to fit the chair seat.

Step 6:

Fold the top of the seat fabric in two lengthwise. Cut small "v" notches at the folds to mark the center front and center back. When in doubt, always find center.

Step 7:

Use the old boxing piece for the approximate length of the new boxing band. Add enough extra inches to the overall length so that you can shift the boxing right or left for the pattern match. Also, remember that the depth of the new boxing will need to be extended since it was undoubtedly trimmed back after the boxing was stapled to the seat.

Step 8:

Place the newly cut seat top fabric on a flat surface. Line up the new boxing piece right under the front cut edge of the top piece. Shift the boxing piece (right or left) so that the pattern repeat on the fabric top aligns with the boxing pattern.

Step 9:

No matter what kind of pattern you're trying to match, you need to determine where the stitch line will ultimately fall on both pieces in order to create the complete pattern. Mark where the stitch line will be with straight pins. Make sure you include the $1/2"$ seam allowances on both pieces.

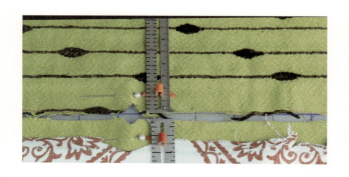
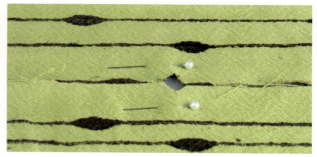

Step 10:

Starting at the notched center of the seat top, pin the boxing onto the seat top, working one direction from the center, then move around the other way. Stop pinning 2" from the center back. Fold one cut edge of the boxing back over itself 1".

Note: Once the band turns the corners of the seat cushion, the pattern matching will be a moot point.

Step 11:

Stitch the boxing to the fabric top, smoothing the fabric as you gradually turn the corners. Stop 2" before connecting the boxing back edges.

Step 12:

Pin the left end of the boxing over the folded-over end of the right side of the boxing, overlapping 2". Stitch all the layers in place on the seam line. Flip the boxing right side up. Pin the back opening closed, keep the fabric pattern lined up, and topstitch the seam closed.

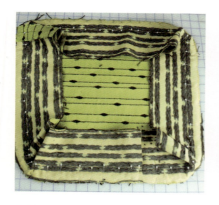

Step 13:

Remove pins and make $1/4''$ long clips straight into the seam allowance around the corners. This releases the fabric so that it lies smooth. Trim the seam allowance to $1/4''$ around the corners if it's bulky. Press finished seat covering with seam allowances downward toward boxing. Fold the seat cover in two to determine the center points. Make a "v" notch at the center of the bottom of the boxing.

Step 14:

Pull the seat cover down over the padded seat, aligning the center front and back of the fabric cover to the seat base. Adjust the covering so that the stitched covering is even and snugly down on the padding.

Step 15:

Determine what the final depth of the boxing will be so that the cover fits smoothly and snugly on the seat base. Measure and mark that boxing depth all around the seat.

Step 16:

Use the four-point stapling method, beginning in the center front, then center back, center left, and center right, using 4–5 staples on each side, alternating and moving out to within 3" from the corners.

Step 17:

Use your hand to smooth and ease in the fabric around the corners so there's no puckering. Staple the corner fabric in place. Trim excess fabric and add a dustcover to the bottom. Reattach chair bottom to the frame.

Back Panels

Step 18:

Trace and cut new 1" foam for inside back and outside back panels. Use adhesive to secure foam onto wood panels.

Step 19:

Pad the top of each foam panel with cotton batting. Feather the edges just like we did on the seat.

Step 20:

Use ¼" staples since the wood panel is thin. Attach the fabric to the front panel, using the standard four-point upholstery technique. To create crisp folded corners, establish where the corner folds will fall. Cut the excess fabric out from behind the fold and create a sharp fold line on the edge of the panels. Staple snugly in place.

Step 21:

Place the upholstered panel on top of the chair frame. Use small carpentry nails at six evenly distributed points around the outside edge of the chair panel. Lightly tap the nails through the fabric, padding, and panel wood and into the chair frame. When the nail head is flush with the fabric, use the pincers to push down just a little bit and clip off the nail head. The fabric springs back up over the clipped-off nail shaft, hiding the nail.

Step 22:

Repeat step 21 for the back panel of the chair.

Project 3:
LEATHER-TRIMMED
VALET BENCH REMODEL

The thrill of coming home has never changed.

—Guy Pearce, Australian actor and musician

Once you acquire the skills that enable you to create a signature piece of furniture that appeals to many, as well as a product design that can be sold over and over again, it could be time to test the market to see if there's a demand for your designs. I found this to be a clever and efficient way to help finance my budding business. It's smart and it's fun.

Start by looking around and paying attention to what kinds of benches your market is buying, learn what fabric designs are trending, and then amp it up a few notches to grab the attention of style-savvy customers and boutique shops.

This project, an out-of-date, upholstered, scroll-armed parsons bench, desperately needed a complete remodel and makeover. It took only a few specialized tools and a little bit of practical carpentry know-how to completely redesign this castoff into a fresh, modern bench suitable to any room in the house. Benches scream versatility!

Skills

Basic carpentry (measuring and cutting off arm scrolls)
Creating new top rails for arms
Sanding legs with a palm sander
Padding the redesigned bench
Creating leather welt cord
Creating a boxed and corded cushion cover
Creating a leather corded fabric band
Sewing decorative leather straps onto fabric
Upholstering the leather-trimmed arm rail band onto the bench
Using cardboard tack strip
Cutting and finishing fabric around a leg rail

Materials and Supplies

Burlap
2" foam
1" foam
Polyester Dacron batting
Main fabric
Contrast fabric for inside and outside arms
Leather straps
Leather hide
Staples
Spray adhesive
Nylon thread
Wood stain for legs
Dustcover for bottom
Nylon thread for hand sewing

Specialty Tools

Reciprocating saw or jigsaw
Electric palm sander
Rotary cutter for cutting fabric and leather
Quilter's ruler for cutting straight lines

What You Do:

Step 1:

Strip down the old parsons bench. Using a small palm sander, sand off the old stain on the legs.

Carpentry

Step 2:

Measure and mark the cutting lines for removing the scroll arms. Use a reciprocating or jigsaw to cut off the scroll. Sand the rough-cut wood with a sanding block or sandpaper.

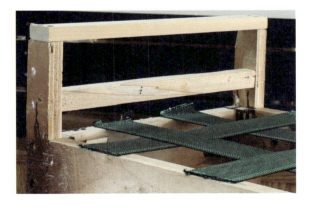

Step 3:

Measure and cut a piece of 1" x 3" wood to create the new top rails for each arm. Mark, drill, and screw the cut wood in place with two $1^3/_4$" screws.

Step 4:

It was necessary to add a slat of wood at the top of the outside arms to even up the vertical arm posts where the scrolls were removed. The new piece will also serve as an attachment rail for the outside arm fabric.

Step 5:

Next, you'll need to begin building the foundation and padding for the inside arms. Stretch three pieces of webbing vertically on each inside arm section.

Step 6:

Measure, cut, and attach a piece of burlap on top of the bench webbing. The burlap should be 1" larger all around than the seat frame. Use the four-point attachment process as shown in the Buttoned-Down Blue Velvet Footstool, step 11. Fold the cut edge over itself and then staple again. Do the same for the inside arm sections.

PRO TIP: When foam is placed on top of burlap-covered webbing, the finished seat can end up looking flat and a bit saggy if there's not some extra height added in the center. A nifty little trick is to cut a piece of 1" foam as a booster piece that measures 3–4" smaller than the top piece, and adhere it right in the center of the seat. The top foam will then look "beefier" in the center, creating a mock crowned-seat shape.

This technique is used on webbed seats with no springs, as well as a flat piece of wood.

Step 7:

Measure, mark, and cut the 1" booster foam for the center of the bench seat. Measure, mark, and cut the 2" top foam, allowing 1/2" overhang all around the seat frame. Spray the adhesive on the burlap and the 1" foam. Center the foam and press in place. Next, spray an ample amount of adhesive all over the glued-down 1" foam and the surrounding burlap base, as well as the underside of the top piece of foam. Carefully place the top foam in place and press down on it or sit on the bench for a few minutes until all foam is adhered.

Step 8:

Measure and cut Dacron batting to cover the bench seat. Make cuts that will allow the Dacron to slide between the arm posts. Pull and smooth the Dacron under the arm rails to the outside of each arm.

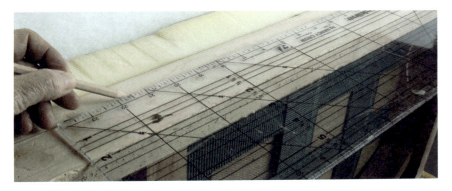

Step 9:

Before pulling and stapling the Dacron batting on the front and back seat rails of the bench, measure and draw a line 2" up from the bottom of the front and back rails. This measurement can vary depending on the bench. Now, pull and smooth the Dacron down over the foam cushion, stapling it at the marked staple line. Smooth the Dacron out and at a diagonal as you staple it in place, moving toward the legs. Trim off the excess Dacron that extends below the marked staple line.

Mini Workshop: Creating Leather Welt Cord

Step 10:

Place leather hide on a flat surface. Cut 1³/₄" strips for single-welt cord.

Step 11:

Create welt cord strips by placing one cut leather strip horizontally on the sewing machine deck, right side up. Place the next piece, right side down, on top of the first piece at a right angle. The two pieces are crisscrossed with right sides together. Turn the two layers slightly to the right in order to stitch the strips together from the upper left to the bottom right. To lock the stitching, use the reverse stitch at the start and finish for 3–4 stitches when sewing the strips together. Trim the seam allowances to $1/2$".

Step 12:

Tuck the $5/32$" welt cord into the inside of the folded leather strips and stitch the cording closed by using a single-welt-cord presser foot or a zipper foot.

Creating the Corded and Boxed

Step 13:

Measure, mark, and cut the top piece of fabric for the boxed bench cover. Cut it out to be the exact width and length, plus $1/2$" all around for seam allowance.

Step 14:

Line up the cut edges of the leather cording with the cut edges of the benchtop fabric. For the visual aesthetic, make sure that none of the cording seams end up right in the center of the front or back of the bench top. Stitch the cording around the fabric top, allowing a ¹/₂" seam allowance. Make clips in the cording seam allowance so it can turn the corners. Make sure that the cording ends will connect on a short end of the bench, where it will be tucked under an arm and not visible.

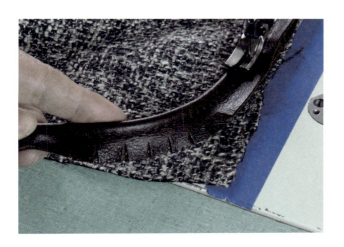

Mini Workshop: How to Connect Welt Cord Ends

Cut the excess cording so that there's a 2" overlap on both sides.

Open up the stitching on one end to expose the tissue-filled cord.

Cut off 1" of the exposed cording, leaving the fabric (leather) covering empty.

Make a chalk line on the other end of the cording and cut the covered cord at that line.

Both ends of the cut cord should meet, with enough fabric on one side to fold under and cover the other cut end.

Stitch the connected welt cord in place.

Step 15:

For the boxing, measure and cut a strip of fabric 6" wide, and long enough to stitch around the benchtop fabric with an added 4" for finishing the ends. This will be the bench cushion boxing. Depending on the necessary boxing length, two additional 6" wide pieces may have to be stitched to the main piece to obtain the right length.

Adjust the boxing for the best placement in regard to the seams, and pin the boxing to the benchtop fabric. At the point where the boxing ends come together, fold one end back over itself 1½" and then overlap the other cut end on top of the folded end. Stitch the boxing onto the top, right side to right side, with the cording sandwiched between the two layers.

Step 16:

Turn the covering right side out and press. Pin and topstitch the back seam closed ⅛" from the folded edge. Next, you'll want to line up the center point on the boxing front with the center point of the bench frame front. Do the same for the back. Place the top cover over the cushion.

Step 17:

Fold the two side ends over themselves and create the standard cuts that will allow the short ends of the cover to be pulled through the end posts. Straighten and adjust the covering. Add a little polyester stuffing up in the corners to fill them out.

Step 18:

Measure the distance from the top piece of cording to where the boxing will be attached to create a snug, tight, and smooth fabric top. Pencil that line, which will be slightly below the stapled Dacron line. As a handy gauge, measure and cut a piece of cardboard tack strip the exact distance from the leather cord to fabric staple line. Begin stapling in the center and move out toward the corners, smoothing with your hand downward and at a diagonal, using the cardboard for your ruler and attaching the staples below the Dacron line.

Corded Band

Step 19:

To create the corded bands that will be attached on the front and back rails under the boxing, cut two 5" wide strips of fabric 4" longer than the bench width. Stitch the leather cording on the top of each band, positioning the cording so that the seams don't fall right in the center of the bench rails.

Step 20:

Measure and mark the horizontal line where the cording will be attached on the front rail. On this bench, it's 2" from the bottom of the rails.

Step 21:

Flip the corded band upside down on the chalked line, with the seam allowances facing downward. Place the cardboard tack strip on top of seam allowance, making sure the cording stays straight and equidistant from the bottom edge all the way across. Staple the band in place by attaching staples diagonally across the tack strip.

Step 22:

Now add a 2" wide piece of Dacron batting across the top of the tack strip. Add a few staples to hold it in place. Pull the band down over the Dacron and under the front and back rails. Pull, smooth, and staple the band in place on the bottom of the rails, starting in the center and moving outward toward the legs.

PRO TIP: You'll need to open up the stitched cord and remove the cord that extends beyond the cushion in order to flatten the cording and attach the band to the arm rail.

Step 23:

Finish the band fabric by making an angled cut from the bottom edge up to the frame and leg intersection. Fold the band fabric up and under the rail and attach.

Trim the excess band fabric to ³/₄" from the legs.

Inside Arms

Step 24:

Measure, cut, and attach 1" foam to the inside arms. Attach Dacron batting over the foam.

Step 25:

Attach the inside arm fabric on top of the arm rail and down the front and back of that rail. Make appropriate cuts for fabric to thread between arm posts. An angled fold is created just below the intersection of the front rail and arm/leg post. Pull and staple the inside arm fabric to the inside rail of the outside arm.

Leather-Embellished Arm Top

This fabric piece runs across the top of the arm rail, including the front and back of that rail. We've added a stitched leather strap for tailored detail. This piece has to be placed just right so that the leather is centered evenly across the top, front, and back of the arm rail when stapled in place.

Step 26:

Measure, mark, and cut the fabric that will cover the top rail of the arm. Place fabric on the top rail to determine where the inside edge of the fabric will be attached and where the leather strap will be stitched in place. Use temporary spray adhesive to hold the leather straps in place for stitching.

Step 27:

Topstitch the leather band on the top rail fabric.

Step 28:

Use a pencil to mark (on the underside) where the leather-detailed top rail fabric will be attached on the inside of the top rails with cardboard tack strip.

Step 29:

Carefully place the topstitched fabric piece upside down, using cardboard tack strip along the inside of the top rail of the arm.

Step 30:

Attach a 2" wide piece of Dacron batting right on top of the cardboard tack strip and across the rail top. Now roll the fabric over to cover the arm, making sure the leather is centered on the arm top, front, and back. Pull and smooth the fabric firmly and evenly and attach it on the outside of the arm.

Outside Arms

Step 31:
For fun, create a dated time capsule to place inside one of the outside arms.

Step 32:
Measure, cut, and attach a piece of burlap to close the outside arm openings.

Step 33:
Measure and cut a piece of the finish fabric 3" larger all around for the outside arms. For a finished surface 17" x 9", I cut the fabric 20" x 12".

Flip the outside arm fabric upside down, as in step 21. Place a piece of cardboard tack strip across the top and attach with staples installed at a diagonal. Cut and attach a piece of Dacron on top of the tack strip and ½" inside the outside edges of the bench.

Step 34:

Flip the fabric over the Dacron covering. Pull the fabric down snugly in the center and install a temporary staple in the center under the bottom rail. Trim the sides of the fabric panel $3/4"$ wider than each outside arm.

Step 35:

Remove the temporary staple and now smooth and pull the fabric down and outward toward the legs, then attach staples under the bottom rail, stopping 2" short of each leg.

Step 36:

Fold both side edges of the outside arm fabric under $1/2"$ and smooth and pin snugly in place.

Step 37:

Make an angled cut from the bottom edge of the fabric up to the juncture of the bottom rail and the leg. Cut the fabric "tab" that is created over the leg to $3/4"$ on top of the leg. Fold that cut tab up and under, creating a finished bottom edge of fabric on the leg. Pin fabric snugly in place at the corner.

Step 38:
Staple the remaining fabric across the bottom rail.

Step 39:
Hand-stitch all pinned sections closed by using the upholsterer's invisible stitch.

Mini Workshop: Upholsterer's Invisible Hand Stitching

Learning how to close up fabric openings with this stitch is a necessity when doing upholstery. Sometimes it's called a ladder stitch or a suture stitch. The gist is that two pieces of fabric are stitched together with a completely invisible stitch. It's high end and quite crafty.

Step 40:
Thread a curved needle with nylon or heavy-duty thread with a knot in one end.

Step 41:
Bury the knot at the top of one pinned side.

Step 42:
Run the thread downward approximately 1/4" inside the fabric or fold.

Step 43:
Bring the needle back out from behind the fabric and move the needle straight across to the other pinned side. Repeat step 42. Move back and forth from side to side, keeping the thread entering and exiting behind the folded edge. The key is to exit one side and enter the other side directly across from where the needle and thread exited. When finished, make a double knot and cut off the excess thread.

Step 44:
Measure, cut, and staple a dustcover on the bottom of the bench.

Project 4:

LOW-SLUNG MIDCENTURY MODERN LOUNGER

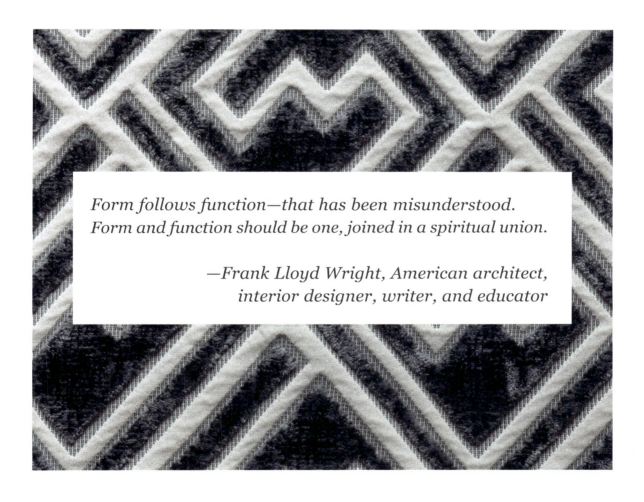

*Form follows function—that has been misunderstood.
Form and function should be one, joined in a spiritual union.*

*—Frank Lloyd Wright, American architect,
interior designer, writer, and educator*

An iconic mid-twentieth-century lounger is chock-full of upholstery skills you'll need to expand your business. And you don't have to love this vintage style in order to appreciate the fact that a well-done modern chair adds a big dollop of delightful interest to an eclectic space. The clean lines of this chair are pleasingly unobtrusive; a piece like this can add the much-needed "friction" to a room's decor with unexpected color or pattern. When tackling a fully upholstered chair for a complete makeover, it helps to break the work down into manageable chunks. Here's what we have:

Foundation/deck (the flat surface underneath a loose cushion)
Front band or nose (the fabric that is stitched to the decking and covers the area
    right under the cushion)
Inside back
Inside arms with mini wings
Outside arms
Outside back
Boxed and corded cushion
Hand stitching
Dustcover

Skills

Creating a padded deck for the cushion base
Padding an entire chair frame
Making a boxed and corded cushion
Making proper cuts for inside frame rails
Pattern matching all pieces
Inside arms and mini wings matched, stitched, and upholstered in place

Materials and Supplies

3" soft foam for inside back
Jute twine
Dacron batting
Cotton batting
Nylon thread
Webbing
Burlap
Decking fabric
Spray adhesive for foam

Specialty Tools

Small level to keep the plaid straight vertically and horizontally
Curved needle
Sewing machine with a single-welt-cord foot

What You Do:

Step 1:

Tear down armchair in this order, labeling each piece and taking photos as you go.

Dustcover
Unhook bottom rail staples or tacks
Outside back
Outside arms
Inside arms
Inside back
Front nose and cushion deck

Not surprisingly, the new fabric will go back on the chair in the reverse order.

Step 2:

Make all necessary frame repairs and reinforcements before starting the reupholstery process.

Step 3:

If you need to tighten the sinuous (zigzag) springs, anchor a piece of jute twine to one side rail either by stapling or by attaching two tacks approximately ½" apart and looping the twine around the tacks and pounding them flush with the rail. Run the twine across the vertically attached springs and tie a half knot on each spring as you pull it taut. Pull the remaining twine taut and attach it to the opposite rail. Sinuous springs need only one or two ties across the rails.

Step 4:

Stretch webbing vertically across inside arm openings.

Step 5:

Attach burlap snugly over inside back springs, seat springs, and newly webbed inside arms.

Step 6:

Place a thick layer of cotton batting on top of the seat burlap as a barrier against the spring abrasion. Then add a layer of Dacron batting on top of the cotton.

Step 7:

In order to establish the plaid placement right off the bat for matching, wrap the fabric around the old cushion in order to determine the plaid placement for all remaining pieces.

Step 8:

Use the old pattern to cut a piece of decking fabric. Also, cut the nose fabric deep enough (12" here) to stitch to the decking fabric and to wrap it around the "nose" and the bottom of the front rail.

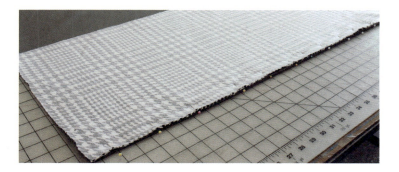

Step 9:

Measure, mark, and cut a 3" piece of foam to pad the inside back. Cut the foam long enough so that it slightly rolls over the center top rail, wide enough to just tuck between the inside back and the inside arm rails, and long enough to tuck down between the inside back and the seat deck. Bevel off the sharp corners of the front side of the foam at a 45° angle.

Step 10:

Place a thick layer of cotton batting on top of the inside back burlap. This is to protect the foam from the spring friction. Feather off the edges with your fingers and place a few staples in the cotton to hold the cotton on the top rail.

Step 11:
Roll the top of the inside back foam over and staple it in place across the top rail.

Step 12:
Cover the inside back with a piece of Dacron batting, making proper cuts for the upper and lower rails.

Step 13:
Use the plaid placement on the fabric-wrapped seat cushion to determine the plaid placement for the inside back. Measure and cut a piece of fabric for the inside back. Use a level to ensure that the plaid is level horizontally and vertically prior to attaching.

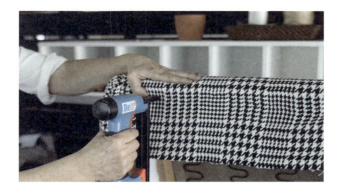

Step 14:
    Start to attach the inside back fabric, starting on the center back of the top rail. Pull and smooth, moving out toward the edges.

Step 15:
    Carefully snip the IB fabric to wrap snugly around the top rail and bottom rails. Before attaching the remaining IB fabric, use the level to check the plaid alignment.

Step 16:
    Tuck all pieces through the rails from front to back. Temporarily tack those fabric pieces on the rails, facing inward until later.

Creating a Boxed and Corded Cushion Cover

A boxed and corded cushion consists of five parts. The simplest way to make a boxed cushion is to measure, cut, and sew each of the required pieces, and then to assemble the cushion. Here's what you need:

- 1 top and 1 bottom piece of fabric cut 1/2" larger all around than the cushion
- Fabric-covered welt cording (piping)
- Front and side boxing strips cut 1" wider than the cushion depth and 4" longer than the front of the cushion plus the length of each cushion side
- Zipper boxing (2" wider than the boxing strip, and 4" longer than the finished zipper length)

Top and Bottom of Cushion

Step 17:

For this tricky plaid, marking and maintaining center is crucial for the success of the cushion. You can use the old cushion as a pattern if it has maintained its shape. I usually take the entire cushion apart to use the top piece as a template.

Position the old pattern on the new plaid fabric and carefully cut out the top of the cushion. Remember, you've already decided on the pattern placement. Cut a small center "v" notch in the front and back of the top piece of the cushion. Flip that piece over on another section of fabric so that the pattern is identical. Right side to right side, cut out the bottom of the cushion.

Cording

Step 18:

Measure around the cushion top and multiply that length by 2, and then add 4" more for each cord connection. Since the plaid is busy, I decided to cut the fabric strips on the straight grain of the fabric and match the plaid on the front of the cushion.

Cut 1³/₄" wide fabric strips for single-welt cord. Stitch welt cording as explained in the "Mini Workshop: Creating Leather Welt Cord" in Project 3.

Boxing

Use the old boxing and zipper sections to estimate the lengths of each section. Always add a few extra inches to the length of each measurement for adjustments.

Step 19:

Plaids on the cushion top and bottom must match the plaid on the center front of the boxing fabric. Cut the boxing fabric 1" wider than the cushion depth. To create enough length of the front boxing strip, cut another identical piece of boxing, then cut it in half and stitch each cut half to the short ends of the front boxing strip, matching the plaids, of course.

Zipper

Creating this zipper section is a little bit more challenging with the plaid, since the plaid will need to match not only the cushion top and bottom, but also the center where the zipper is installed.

To make it simple, measure the length of the zipper piece from the old cushion.

Cut each of the zipper fabric pieces so that the full plaid design is at one edge. This way, you'll have plenty of room to adjust and pin the two lengths together for basting, so that the full plaid design will wind up right in the center of the zipper boxing.

The finished boxing is 3", so the cut boxing measures 4" wide. However, for the zipper, I cut the two zipper section pieces (top and bottom) 4" wide. The finished zipper boxing width will be trimmed even with the width of the main boxing piece after the zipper is stitched to the top and bottom sections.

Step 20:

Place the top and bottom of the zipper boxing pieces together so that the full plaid patterns are aligned. Fold both of those edges under so that both of those halves create one full plaid pattern visible from the right side. Pin the folds in place and then press the folds in place. Now, pin and baste the zipper section pieces together. For a plain fabric, you just need at least a 1" seam allowance on both sides to install the zipper. Press the seam open and use temporary spray adhesive to hold the zipper in place.

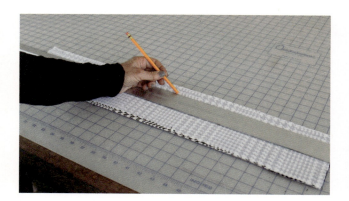

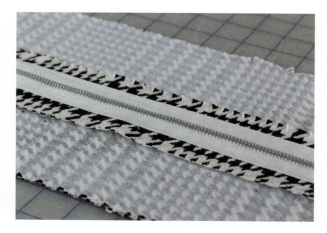

Step 21:

Stitch the zipper in place from the right side of the zipper section. Hold the zipper firmly in the center of the seam while you're stitching. Stitch straight down each side, lock stitching (forward three stitches, reverse three stitches) at the start and finish of each line of stitching.

Step 22:

Open the basting seam enough to slide the zipper pull onto the teeth. Stitch fabric tabs in place on the top of the zipper boxing section and at the other end of the zipper boxing section. Now the zipper section is prepared.

All the cushion pieces are ready for assembly.

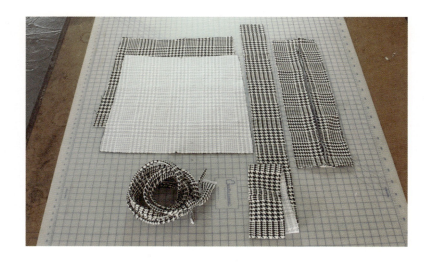

Cushion Assembly

Step 23:

Stitch the fabric-covered cording to the top and bottom of the cushion pieces, starting in the center front and connecting the cording in the center back. See the Mini Workshop in Project 3 on connecting cording (page 101).

Step 24:

With center notches of the boxing and the cushion top aligned, use a regular stapler to temporarily attach the boxing to the cushion top. The stapler allows you to keep the plaids lined up. Stitch the main boxing piece to the cushion top, starting in the center and stitching around to within 4" from the back corner of the cushion. Flip the fabric over and, starting again in the center, stitch around the other side to within 4" from the other corner. Clip straight into the boxing at the corners to allow close stitching right up to the cording.

Step 25:

Cut "v" notches in the unstitched boxing edge at the two front side corners. Line up the notches with the corners of the cushion bottom.

Step 26:

Repeat step 24 for the bottom of the cushion.

Step 27:

To install the zipper boxing, line up the center back notch on the cushion top with the notch in the center of the zipper section, matching plaids. Staple the two pieces together and stitch in place, stopping 2" before reaching the back corners of the cushion. Repeat this for the cushion bottom.

Now pin the short ends of the zipper boxing to the short ends of the front boxing piece. Stitch the ends closed using $1/2$" seam allowance.

Step 28:

Now pin the remaining unstitched zipper boxing around the back corners, slightly overlapping the zipper boxing onto the folded back piece of the front boxing. Stitch the seams closed. The zipper boxing should now be completely installed, and the cushion cover completed. It's helpful to trim the seam allowance at the stitched corners.

The plaids on the inside back and the cushion cover are lined up. It's time to get the front band and decking attached. If your fabric doesn't have a pattern match, the decking and front band would be the first piece to go on the chair.

Deck and Front Band

Step 29:

Place the stitched deck and nose fabric on the Dacron-covered seat deck. Use the level to check the plaid alignment on the nose before anchoring the deck/nose seam to the burlap. Use nylon tufting twine, a curved needle, and a basic running stitch to anchor the decking seam allowance to the burlap along with the spring edges as you stitch the deck in place. "Catching" the springs in your stitches prevents movement and unwanted friction of the deck on the springs. At each end, pull the twine down to the frame and staple the ends in place, then fold the twine over itself and staple again.

Step 30:

Place the reusable cotton onto the front rail, adding extra cotton batting to freshen up the front rail padding. Flip the nose fabric over and make the proper rail cuts to fit snugly around the front arm rails.

Step 31:

Fold the seat deck fabric back over itself at a 45° angle to the vertical back corner posts (there are two rails the fabric must wrap around). Make proper cuts and pull the fabric through under the inside back and inside side rails. Starting in the center back, staple the deck fabric smoothly in place, moving toward the corners. Repeat this decking attachment on both sides.

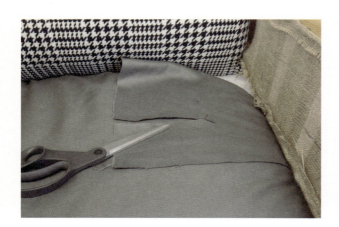
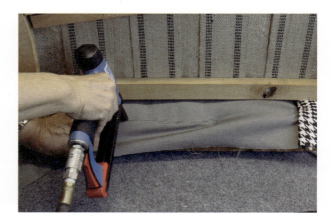

Step 32:

Measure, cut, and attach ½" foam on the inside arms, making the proper cuts to allow the foam to wrap around the rails. Cut a second piece of foam to cover the "mini wing" on the inside arm. This piece has to have an inside cut to fit through the inside rails.

Step 33:

Attach Dacron batting to the inside arms.

Inside Arm and Mini Wing Fabric

The inside arm is made up of two pieces of fabric: the mini wing and the lower inside arm. The important thing on the arms is to have the plaid match in two places: across the cushion and above the seam on the mini wing. In order to achieve this, place the old fabric pieces on top of the arm and make a mark across the seam on both pieces for a stitching guide.

Step 34:

On the curved stitch line where the arm meets the mini wing, cut corresponding notches for proper matching. Pin and stitch the two pieces together and then check out the match and fit on the chair arm.

Step 35:
Clip the curved seam allowance to allow snug fitting on the arm curve.

Step 36:
Fit the inside arm fabric onto the chair, matching the plaids and making all the proper rails cuts, both on the seat deck and on the mini wing so that the arm fits nice and snugly on the inside arm. Pull the inside arm / wing piece around the top of the arm, anchor it at the seam on the outside frame, and clip the fabric at the curve in order to release it.

Step 37:
Make a neat corner on the front of the inside arm rails. See corners in Project 1, step 21 (page 80).

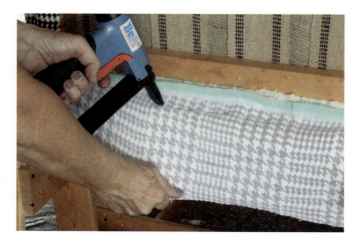

Step 38:
Pull the inside arm fabric down and through the lower arm rails. Pull, smooth, and attach the fabric to the top of the lower back rail.

Step 39:

It's time to do the final smoothing and stapling of the inside chair fabrics that need to be attached to the chair rails from the outside of the chair. All the flaps that were temporarily attached inward should now be pulled and attached on the rails, facing outward. This seals the inside of the chair from dirt and debris falling into the interior. Trim excess fabric so that it's nice and tidy looking.

Step 40:

Before closing up any chair, I always include a time capsule for the next upholsterer.

Step 41:

Cut and attach a piece of burlap to close in the outside arms. Next, attach Dacron to the outside arm, stapled $1/2$" inside the edge all around.

Step 42:

Place the old fabric on top of the outside arm.

Step 43:

Mark where the plaid pattern will need to match the front arm and top arm rail.

Step 44:

Pin the OA in place and use the level, both horizontally and vertically.

Step 45:

Cut the OA fabric to fit the arm. The inside curves need to be clipped to "release" the fabric so that it relaxes and conforms to the curves. Leave 1/2" to 3/4" allowance for folding the edge under and hand stitching it in place.

Step 46:

Pin and hand-stitch the top of the OA in place, using the upholsterer's invisible stitch. Pull the fabric firmly and staple the fabric under the bottom rail. Smooth and pull the OA around the back of the frame and staple it in place. Check the plaid as you staple.

Step 47:

Cut out a fabric piece for the back that is large enough to adjust for the plaid match.

Step 48:

Attach the OB fabric by flipping it upside down and attaching it by using cardboard tack strip and diagonally placed staples. See Project 3, step 21. Leave $3/4$" unstapled on both top edges for folding under and hand stitching.

Flip the OB fabric down over the back and attach a temporary staple in the center bottom. Now trim both edges, leaving $3/4$" on both sides for folding under and hand stitching closed. We're not stitching just yet. Check the pattern match again.

Step 49:

Remove the staples from the bottom of the OB. Flip the OB fabric piece back over. Attach a piece of polyester Dacron right on top of the cardboard tack strip and covering the entire OB, leaving $1/2$" free of Dacron on both side edges. This will leave room for clean hand stitching with no Dacron interference.

Step 50:

Find the center of the chair bottom and the center of the plaid alignment, then put an anchor staple under the bottom rail in the center.

Step 51:

Now, pin and stitch the sides closed, keeping the plaid perfectly aligned.

Step 52:

Remove the anchor staple and now firmly pull, smooth, and attach the back piece under the bottom rail, moving out from the center toward the corners.

Step 53:

Hand-stitch any remaining openings closed, using the upholsterer's invisible stitch.

Step 54:

Attach a dustcover on the bottom of the chair, using the standard four-point stapling technique. Attach the furniture legs.

Project 5:

ROCKIN' MOROCCAN
HANGING HEADBOARD

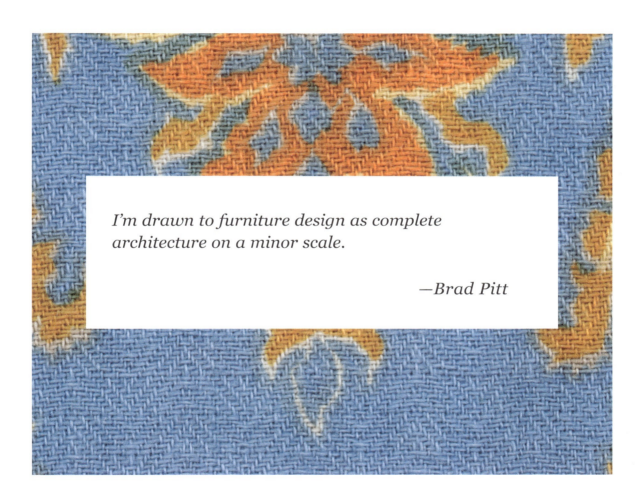

I'm drawn to furniture design as complete architecture on a minor scale.

—Brad Pitt

Relatively simple, yet having visual impact, this shapely chartreuse hanging-headboard project includes skill builders you can use to create custom headboards or an entire line of your own designs. You will soon be creating bespoke bedheads that yield high profit margins for you and your business. Fancy shapes and decorative details are add-on luxuries that enable you to realize even more profitability. I recommend adding all kinds of styles of upholstered headboards to your offerings. They can turn into a cash cow for your new business, since upholstered headboards are relatively simple to create and they never go out of style.

But brace yourself. Before you know it, friends and customers will soon ask you to create custom headboards for them. This project requires you to expand your new upholstering skills to include simple frame building. It's not hard—I'll help you.

Skills

Enlarging a small projected image onto a piece of wood
Using a jigsaw or a reciprocating saw to cut a curvy shape
Carpentry-simple frame building
Upholstering a complex shape
Attaching a French cleat

Materials and Supplies

1 piece of $^3/_4$" x 4' x 68" plywood
Scrap strips of 2' x 10" x $^3/_4$" plywood
2" x 2" and 2" x 4" cut chunks of 2" x 4"
1$^3/_4$" wood screws
1 piece of 1" x 6" x 53" plywood (used for a necessary extension on the bottom of the headboard; it will be the same width as the bottom width of your headboard frame)
2 large pieces of 1" foam
Jute webbing
Burlap
Polyester Dacron
Cardboard tack strip
Wool felt or polyester felt for batting
1 long or 2 medium-length French cleat hanging hardware

Specialty Tools

Reciprocating saw or jigsaw
Palm sander

ALWAYS WEAR SAFETY GLASSES WHEN YOU'RE USING POWER TOOLS!

What You Do:

Step 1:
Use a projector to trace the headboard shape onto a piece of $^3/_4$" plywood.

Step 2:
In order to create a dimensional headboard, the Moroccan shape needs to be cut out of two pieces of plywood. To eliminate some of the extra weight, we attached scrap pieces of plywood on top of the full piece of plywood on top of the traced outline with 1$^3/_4$" screws. Use a jigsaw or reciprocating saw to cut out the traced shape.

Step 3:
Smooth off the cut edge using a palm sander.

Step 4:

Mark and attach metal braces to connect the duplicated scrap wood pieces in order to create one continuous piece of the headboard outline.

Step 5:

The two layers of wood will be separated by wood blocks in order to create a dimensional frame. Before separating the two layers, mark the two attached plywood pieces around the cut edges at 10"–12" intervals in order to keep the pieces aligned when constructing the final frame.

Step 6:

Create a line across the back of the wood frame, using a level and a long metal yardstick. Place the spacer blocks evenly around the back side of the cut frame.

Step 7:

Since the headboard is so heavy, I got down on the floor and drilled holes from the front side into the spacer blocks and attached the blocks with 1$\frac{1}{2}$" screws.

Step 8:

Line up the duplicate frame on top of the spacer blocks and screw it into the spacer blocks.

Step 9:

Trace, cut, and attach an extension piece of wood that will be covered with fabric to slide behind the mattress when the headboard is installed.

We now have the headboard frame prepared. However, it was too heavy to carry, much less hang on the wall. I had to make an adjustment. I decided to cut out a large rectangle from the center of the front piece to lighten the load.

Step 10:

I traced a rectangle on the front solid piece of wood and drilled a large hole at the corner of the traced rectangle large enough for a jigsaw blade to fit through. Cut out the traced rectangle.

Step 11:

Weave jute webbing across the rectangular opening. Attach a piece of burlap on top of the webbing by using the standard four-point stapling technique.

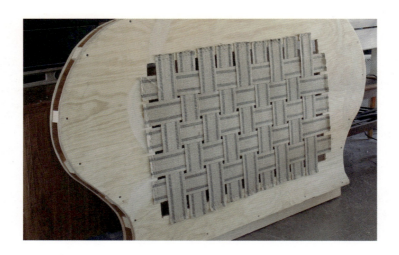

Step 12:

Cut burlap strips 2" wider than the headboard edge and long enough to cover the entire outside edge of the headboard. Starting at the top center, attach the burlap all around to close in the side opening. Fold the burlap back over itself and staple it neatly in place.

The size of this headboard (fits a queen-size mattress) requires two slabs of 1" foam. I chose 1" foam since I've created a 3½" frame and will add Dacron on top of the foam.

Step 13:

Glue two slabs of 24" wide foam together by stacking them on top of each other, with the two long edges aligned. Spray adhesive on those edges and carefully flip the top piece down so that the glued edges meet. Pinch the two edges together until they're strongly adhered.

Step 14:
Trace the headboard shape on the foam and cut it out with an electric knife or foam cutter.

Step 15:
Spray the foam adhesive evenly on the burlap and the underside of the foam. Center and press the foam in place.

Step 16:
Cut a big piece of polyester Dacron 2" larger than the headboard all around. Trim the Dacron so that it extends beyond the headboard by $1/2$". Gently pull the top layer of Dacron apart so that you can staple the bottom layer on the edge of the headboard, compressing the foam at the edges. Allow the top layer of Dacron to cover the stapled "dimples" created by the staples. This allows the Dacron to stay in place but keeps the surface even and smooth. Trim off excess Dacron so that it's flush with the front edge.

Step 17:
Now it's time to cut out the fabric. Since you have no pattern, you'll want to measure and cut the fabric so that it extends amply over the entire outside edge of the frame. Leave enough fabric on the bottom edge to cover the wood extension that will tuck in behind the bed.

Step 18:
Since this is a very curvaceous headboard and the fabric will have to be carefully cut and pulled in order to fit snugly around the front curves of the headboard, make perpendicular cuts into the outside fabric edge, deep enough to allow the fabric to "release" so that it can be manipulated around the tricky inside curves and the bulbous outside curves. Be careful not to cut the fabric so deep that it's visible on the front of the headboard.

Step 19:

Begin attaching the fabric at the center top of one side. Use your hand to smooth and pull the fabric evenly and firmly as you staple. The inside curves are tricky to keep smooth. It takes patience and a willingness to remove staples and try again. This kind of fabric manipulation provides lots of information on how fabric responds to different directional pulling. It teaches you how to find the right place to smooth out dimples or wrinkles. Don't expect it to be perfect the first time.

Step 20:

Make a nice and tidy corner at the bottom edge of the headboard, where the padded top meets the unpadded extension piece of wood. You'll finish that up later.

Step 21:

Measure and cut strips of fabric 5" wide by the total distance around the headboard edge from the bottom of one side to the bottom of the other side. To get a length longer than the 54" wide cut of fabric, cut a second strip measuring 54", cut it in two, and stitch each 27" long piece on either end of the 54" piece.

Cut a "v" notch in the center of the long strip, press the seam allowances open, and use a pencil on the wrong side of the fabric strip to draw a line measuring $1/2$" from the long cut edge of one side of the strip. This is a guide mark to use when stapling the strip to the outside edge of the headboard.

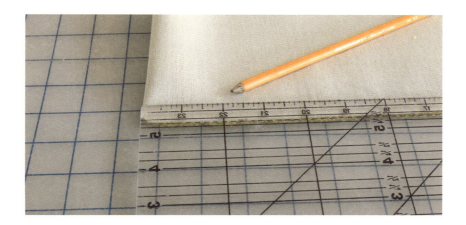

Step 22:

Line up the "v" notch with the top center point of the headboard, with the penciled line aligned evenly with the front edge of the headboard. Attach the strip all around, stapling on the penciled guideline, until you get to the bottom edge. Leave 2" free at the bottom edge of the headboard frame, before the extension piece. Repeat this for the other side, starting at the center top.

Step 23:

Repeat this process, using cardboard tack strip and staples attached on the diagonal. The top edge of the cardboard tack strip should be aligned with the pencil line.

Step 24:

Cut a strip of wool felt or cotton batting the exact width of the headboard edge and attach it at the top edge of the cardboard tack strip. This padding is less lofty than polyester Dacron, so it will provide a little bit of padding but not be too puffy. If you want a puffier edge, use polyester Dacron.

Step 25:

Flip the side band fabric over the wool felt. Start at the center top and work around, alternating from side to side until you reach the bottom edges. It may take some work to keep the fabric taut and smooth on the inside curves and angles. Be patient.

Step 26:

Fold the bottom edge of fabric strip under 1" before stapling the remaining fabric strip snugly on back of the headboard. Clip the inside curves to release the fabric for a smooth finish.

Step 27:

Hand-stitch the bottom edges of the fabric strip closed.

Step 28:

Cut a 54" x 6" strip of fabric to cover the extension piece of wood. Use the cardboard tack strip technique and finish up the edges so they're nice and tidy. No padding is necessary under this strip of fabric. The extension piece needs to be finished with fabric.

Step 29:

Place the headboard upright on a level surface. Determine the height of the metal hanging cleat. Use a level to draw a line across the back of the headboard. Now, attach a piece of 1" x 4" wood across the back of the frame. Use the level again to attach the cleat hanger.

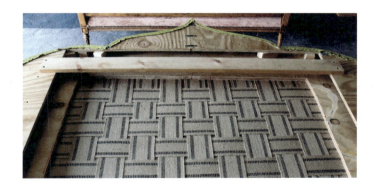

Step 30:

Carefully cut out dustcover fabric to cover the plywood back of the headboard. Leave the center open for easier lifting.

Step 31:

Attach a French cleat (either made from wood or purchased from the hardware store) and hang the headboard.

Chapter Seven

YOU'RE READY

Now you possess the basic upholstery skills that will take you a long way in this new adventure. The time will come when you'll be hungry to learn more-advanced skills and techniques. The search for more training will be a natural evolution of your curiosity and passion. Learn all you can, and get to know the global upholstery community. Upholstering in a shop by yourself can be lonely work. The new upholsterers have discovered that connecting with like-minded artisans around the globe has brought about a camaraderie that didn't exist not so very long ago.

Many upholsterers are traveling to other countries to meet up and share their talents. Medieval craftsmen were linked by the commonality of their shared skills. Today, we still feel a bond with others who share the love of our craft. Enjoy it, let it take you to new places, let it enable you to meet new people, and let it make you want to share it with others.

Deep-buttoned bench designed and created by Paul Behen, owner of Industrial Cottage, Chicago, Illinois